The Lady Vanishes

£1-50

Ethel Lina White

The Lady Vanishes

Adapted by
Jennifer Brain

Oxford University Press

Oxford University Press, Walton Street, Oxford OX2 6DP
Oxford   New York   Toronto
Melbourne   Auckland   Petaling Jaya   Singapore
Hong Kong   Tokyo   Delhi   Bombay   Calcutta   Madras
Karachi   Nairobi   Dar es Salaam   Cape Town

and associated companies in
Beirut   Berlin   Ibadan   Nicosia

OXFORD is a trade mark of Oxford University Press

ISBN 0 19 424224 2

First published in Great Britain 1936 as *The Wheel Spins*
This adapted edition by arrangement with Hamish Hamilton
© Oxford University Press 1980

First published 1980
Third impression 1986

The Lady Vanishes

1000 headword level

Set in Great Britain by
Cox & Wyman Ltd, Reading
Typeset in Intertype Garamond
Printed in Hong Kong

I

Iris Carr had her first feeling of danger the day before it happened. She was usually safe in a crowd of people she called her 'friends'. Her parents were dead, and she had money of her own. There were always people around her. They thought for her, and she accepted their ideas.

She felt that she was popular. At one time she was going to marry one of the crowd. Her photograph appeared in the newspapers.

She was famous.

Then they decided not to marry. Again her picture was in the papers. Famous again. Perhaps her mother would have smiled or cried at this. But her mother died when she was born.

Iris was very well and happy when she had the first feeling of danger. It was at the end of an unusual health-holiday.

The crowd found a beautiful village in a far corner of Europe. They moved into the only hotel for nearly a month. They climbed up mountains, swam in the lake, and lay in the sun. Indoors, they filled the bar, shouting against the radio. They paid well, so the smiling waiters always came to them first. This angered the other English people at the hotel.

These six people thought that Iris was just like the others in her crowd – rich, young, and useless. Naturally they did not know how good she could be. She always paid the bill when she had lunch with her 'friends'. And she was kind when she noticed people in trouble.

The crowd grew brown, they drank, and were happy. The married couples were all very friendly with the others. So Iris was surprised and hurt when one of the women, Olga, started shouting at her.

'You're trying to steal my husband,' shouted Olga.

Iris was angry. The man seemed lonely, she thought. I was just trying to be kind. *He* started the trouble.

Her friends clearly enjoyed the argument. This made it worse. Iris felt angry with them all. So she decided not to travel back to England with the others. She planned to stay on for two more days alone.

She was still feeling angry on the following day. She went with the crowd to the little railway station. Already they were acting like city people again. They wore fashionable clothes. The husbands and wives were together, with their suitcases and tickets.

The train was going to Trieste. It was full of tourists, all going back to city life. The crowd seemed friendly again. They stood round Iris.

'Are you sure you won't be lonely, darling?'

'Change your mind and come with us.'

They tried to pull her onto the train, in her holiday clothes. She fought to get free. She jumped down just as the train began to pull out of the station.

Laughing, she stood and watched the train till it disappeared.

She was glad that her friends were gone. At last she was alone with the mountains and the silence. A grass-green lake lay below her, shining in the sunlight. The snowy mountain tops reached up into the blue sky. The dark shape of an old castle stood on a hill.

Everywhere was full of colour. The station garden was on fire with red and yellow flowers. The white smoke from the train was blowing past the green hillside.

Iris watched it blow away. She no longer belonged to the crowd. She felt that she never wanted to see them again.

Here, under the wide blue sky, people seemed so small, so unimportant. They came, and they went. They didn't matter.

But a few hours later she wanted her friends more than she wanted any of the wonders of nature.

Iris left the cool valley near to a stone cross, and climbed upwards. She soon got out of the shadow, and the sun was burning hot. But she did not slow down. The anger in her thoughts drove her on. She could not get Olga out of her mind.

Olga. Olga ate her food, used her telephone, drove her car, wore her clothes. She used to think Olga was her friend.

She remembered Olga's husband, and began to run.

I'd never want a man who looks like Mickey Mouse, she thought angrily.

At last she was out of breath. She threw herself down on the grass. She decided not to try to reach the top of the mountain. It got further away as she climbed towards it.

She decided to forget Olga.

'But after this,' she said, 'I'll never help anyone again. I've learned that lesson.'

She smoked a cigarette before the return journey. She could see part of the lake far below, no longer green, but light blue.

Sadly she got to her feet. It was time to go.

Going down was hard work. Her legs began to hurt. She decided to take a shorter way down the hillside. She hurried down the valley. She was thinking of the comforts which were waiting for her. A long cold drink, a hot bath, dinner in bed. She caught sight of the shining water, and began to run.

She turned the corner and then stopped. There were no little wooden houses, no railway station, no hotel.

She realized she was lost. This was not the well-known green lake where she bathed daily. It was pale blue, and a different shape.

There was only one thing to do – to go back to the stone cross.

It was clearly amusing. She managed quite a good laugh. Then she turned and began to walk slowly upwards again.

All around were rocks and stones. There was no grass growing, no sound of a bird.

She was very angry with herself. I thought I knew the mountains, she said to herself. I climbed up here so many times with my friends. But I just followed, she thought, others led. There was always someone else with a map.

She was very tired, and her foot hurt. She felt very low.

7

I've been carried all my life, she thought. I can't even speak the language. I can only sign cheques.

A short, heavy man in old dirty clothes was coming up the road. She called out to him in English, and asked him the way to the village.

He looked at her, then shook his head.

She tried again, more loudly. He still took no notice. He started to walk on. She stood in his way.

She felt quite helpless, like someone whose tongue was cut off. She said the name of the village, and waved her arms in different directions.

He must understand that, unless he's stupid, she thought.

He began to speak in a strange language. Suddenly Iris felt afraid. She had no money. She could not speak the language. Perhaps she was lost for ever.

The man's face looked like something from a bad dream. His skin was shiny. He smelt, because he was hot from his climb.

'I can't understand you,' she cried. 'I can't understand one word. Stop. Oh, *stop*. You'll drive me mad.'

The man heard only strange words. He saw a girl, dressed like a man, thin, with cut dirty legs. She was a stranger. She seemed very excited, and very stupid. She was telling him only half the name of the village. The names of three villages began in the same way. He was trying to explain this to her, and asking for the full word.

At last he shook his head and went on his way. Iris was left alone with the mountains. They hung over her, black and dangerous. They were ready to rain down rocks on her head.

Then suddenly she heard English voices. The honeymoon couple from the hotel came round the corner.

They were both very tall, very good-looking. They never spoke to anyone else. The man had a commanding voice, and held his head very high. The woman had a beautiful face and wore expensive clothes.

They signed the book at the hotel with the name of 'Todhunter'. But that was probably not their real name.

They passed Iris almost without seeing her. The man looked

8

at her, but did not recognize her. His wife never moved her blue eyes from the stony road. She was wearing very high shoes.

She was speaking in a low voice.

'No darling. Not another day. Not even for *you*. We've stayed too . . .'

Iris lost the rest of the sentence. She followed them, a little way behind, because she realized how dirty she looked.

Iris knew the hotel was near. The honeymoon couple never walked far. The mountains looked smaller. They were like a picture postcard again.

Very soon Iris saw the first stone cross. Then she saw the lights of the hotel. She began to think again of a hot bath and dinner. She remembered that she was both tired and hungry.

She was safe again now. But she knew what it was like to feel afraid, helpless, far away from home and friends.

2

The honeymoon couple returned to the hotel. The four other English people staying at the hotel were still sitting in the garden. They were enjoying a rest. It was too dark to write letters, or read. But it was too early to dress for dinner. There were empty cups and plates on one of the tables.

The two Misses Flood-Porter liked to sit down. They did not enjoy hurrying about. They were in their fifties. Both had grey hair, and very good skin.

The skin of the elder – Miss Evelyn – was quite lined. She was nearly sixty. But Miss Rose was only just out of her forties. The younger sister was taller and heavier; her voice was louder, her colour deeper. She was strong-minded, and sometimes spoke sharply to her older sister when playing cards.

Now, at the end of their visit, they were with the Reverend

9

Kenneth Barnes and his wife. The four of them planned to return to England on the same train.

There were iron chairs and tables in the garden, painted bright colours. Miss Flood-Porter looked around her, and thought of her own beautiful home in a country town.

The newspapers said it was raining in England. The garden at home will be looking its best, she thought, with bright green grass and richly coloured flowers.

'I'm looking forward to seeing my garden again,' she said.

'*Our* garden,' said her sister.

'And I'm looking forward to a comfortable chair,' laughed the vicar. 'Ha. Here comes the honeymoon couple.'

He was a friendly person, but he did not call out to them. He knew that they did not like to be spoken to. So he sat and watched them going up the steps into the hotel.

'Good-looking couple,' he said.

'I wonder who they *really* are,' said Miss Flood-Porter. 'I'm certain that there is some mystery about them.'

'So am I,' agreed Mrs Barnes. 'I . . . I wonder if they are really married?'

'Are *you*?' asked her husband quickly.

Her face went pink, and he laughed.

'Sorry, my dear,' he said. 'But isn't it better to believe that we are all what we seem to be? Even vicars and their wives.' He got up from his chair. 'I think I'll walk down to the village.'

'I'm afraid we've made him angry,' said Miss Evelyn Flood-Porter.

'Oh no, it was because of me,' said Mrs Barnes. 'I'm always too interested in other people. But the English don't usually take enough interest in others.'

'That's a very good thing,' broke in Miss Rose.

'Of course. But I often think that a stranger sitting beside me may be in some trouble. Perhaps I could help.'

The sisters looked at her kindly. She was a small woman in her middle forties, with a round face, dark hair, and a sweet smile. Her large brown eyes were both kind and truthful. The sisters knew that she always told the truth.

She liked the sisters. They were good women. And they had a lovely house and garden, and money in the bank. Mrs Barnes knew this. But she was glad that the only man among them was her husband.

She knew how lucky she was. She always used to go on a yearly holiday with other unmarried women. She was a teacher until her fortieth birthday. Then a wonderful thing happened. She had – not only a husband – but a son.

Both she and her husband loved the child very much. They thought of almost nothing else except him. This worried the vicar. The night before they set out on their holiday they were talking about him.

'Yes, he *is* beautiful,' he said, looking down at the sleeping boy. 'But sometimes, I wonder . . .'

'I know what you mean,' said his wife.

'We want this holiday to do us real good. Let us agree not to talk only of Gabriel, while we are away.'

Mrs Barnes agreed. But she still thought of him all the time. He was being looked after by a kind grandmother. But Mrs Barnes still worried about him. She was counting the hours before her return to her son. Miss Flood-Porter was smiling at the thought of seeing her garden. Miss Rose was thinking.

'Why don't people always tell the truth?' she said. 'I can't understand it.'

As she spoke, Iris appeared at the end of the hotel garden. She kept away from the group at the table. But she could hear what they were saying.

'I've never even wanted to say anything untrue,' said Mrs Barnes, in her clear, school-teacher's voice.

That's not true, thought Iris.

She was so tired that she could hardly stand. She longed for the quiet of her room. But she knew she could not climb the stairs without a short rest. She dropped down on an iron chair and closed her eyes.

If anyone speaks to me I'll die, she thought.

The Misses Flood-Porter looked at her coldly. Even kind Mrs Barnes's soft brown eyes held no welcome. The crowd always used to treat her badly.

They acted as if they owned the hotel. They always got their meals first, because they gave the waiters money. The other tourists were angry about it, they thought it was unfair.

The crowd always got the best food, and took the best chairs. They used all the hot bath water.

Even the vicar found it difficult to be kind about them. 'Of course, they're young,' he said. But some of them weren't even very young.

'They drink and make love all the time,' said Mrs Barnes. She was glad when they went. She looked forward to two quiet days with her friends and the wonders of nature.

But they did not all go. This girl was still here – and perhaps there were others. Mrs Barnes remembered Iris with the crowd. She's the pretty one. One of the older men was always following her. And he was married too.

But the girl looked so tired. Mrs Barnes's kind heart soon felt sorry for her.

'Are you left all alone?' she called, in her brightest voice.

Iris jumped. At that moment she certainly didn't want an older person asking questions.

'Yes,' she answered.

'Oh dear, how sad. Aren't you lonely?'

'No.'

'But you're very young to be travelling without friends. Couldn't any of your family come with you?'

'I have none.'

'No family at all?'

'No. Aren't I lucky?'

'Oh,' said the Misses Flood-Porter and looked at each other.

Mrs Barnes became silent. Iris did not want any more questions. So she got to her feet with difficulty. She hurt all over. She managed to get into the hotel, and upstairs to her room.

Mrs Barnes tried to laugh.

'I'm afraid I've made another mistake,' she said. 'She clearly doesn't like me. But it seemed so unkind to take no interest in her.'

'Is she interested in *you*?' asked Miss Rose. 'Or in us? That sort of girl only thinks about herself. I'm sure she never does anything to help anyone.'

There was only one answer to the question. Mrs Barnes was too kind to answer it. She remained silent. She could not say anything untrue.

She did not know what was going to happen in the next twenty-four hours. This girl was going to stand alone against everyone. She would be hurt and afraid and nearly driven mad, trying to save a stranger.

If there really was a person called Miss Froy.

3

Iris had a square mark on her hand. Someone told her once that this meant she was safe from danger. Iris laughed, but she believed it.

Now, as usual, the stars were trying to help her. People tried to be friendly to her during the evening. She would soon need friends.

But she wanted to cut herself off from everyone. They did not like her friends, so she did not like *them*.

She missed the crowd as soon as she entered the sitting-room. It was silent and empty. She walked past empty bedrooms. The blankets were taken off the beds and hung out of the windows.

The crowd never used to change for the evening. One day a lady appeared at dinner in her bathing dress. The Misses Flood-Porter were very angry about it. They always wore dark, expensive evening dresses.

Iris remembered this when she finished her bath. She took an afternoon dress out of her suitcase.

She felt better after the hot bath and rest. But she was lonely. She stood with her hand resting on the hand-rail at the top of the stairs.

The newly-married Mr Todhunter came out of his bedroom. He noticed her standing in her pretty dress.

He did not know who she was. He did not realize that she was the girl lost in the mountains that afternoon. He and his wife took their meals in their own sitting-room. So he never met the crowd.

He stopped and smiled at her.

'Quiet, tonight,' he said. 'A nice change after those terrible noisy people.'

To his surprise, the girl looked coldly at him.

'It *is* quiet,' she said. 'But I miss my friends.'

She walked down the stairs feeling pleased. She was glad that she had made him realize his mistake. But she felt a little uncomfortable.

The crowd knew that the others did not like them. They laughed about it. 'We're not popular with these people,' they said happily. Or, 'They don't really like us.' Iris did not mind, when they were all together. But now she was alone.

She entered the restaurant. It was a big room, with dark blue wall-paper with gold stars. Most of the tables were empty. Only one waiter stood sadly by the door.

In a few days, the hotel would be shut up for the winter. Most of the waiters were already gone.

The remaining visitors did not seem to mind this. The Misses Flood-Porter sat at the same table as the vicar and his wife. They were all happy, laughing and making jokes.

Iris carefully chose a small table in a far corner. She smoked a cigarette, and waited for her food.

Mrs Barnes forgot their earlier talk, and looked at her kindly.

'How pretty that girl looks in a dress,' she said.

'*Afternoon* dress,' said Miss Flood-Porter. 'We always wear evening dresses for dinner, when we're away from home.'

Iris took as long as possible over her meal. She sat by herself. The vicar watched her thoughtfully. His clean-cut face was both strong and kind. His wife told him that Iris wanted to be alone. He understood that feeling. He sometimes felt the same. Sometimes he even wanted to get away from his wife.

Perhaps I should leave the girl alone, he thought. But she looks so tired and sad.

In the end he went over to her. She looked up quickly.

Another, she thought. She usually liked his face. But tonight he was one of the enemies. Terrible noisy people. The words came back to her mind as he spoke.

'Are you travelling back to England alone?' he said. 'Would you like to come with us?'

'When are you going?'

'The day after tomorrow. It's the last fast train of the year.'

'But I'm going tomorrow. Thanks so much.'

'Then I'll wish you a good journey.'

The vicar smiled. She's only just decided that, he thought.

'Do you believe in warning dreams, Mr Barnes?' Miss Rose asked the vicar as he returned. 'Because, last night, I dreamed of a railway crash.'

Iris heard this. She listened for the vicar's answer.

'Would you like to see a photograph of my little son Gabriel?' said a bright voice in Iris's ear.

But Iris did not even look at the photograph. Mrs Barnes felt very hurt. Her face turned red, and she moved away. Iris did not mean to be rude. She was trying to hear the talk about dreams.

'You can say what you like,' said Miss Rose. 'I know I'm right. There are always too many people on the last good train of the year. I'll be glad when I'm safely back in England.'

'But you aren't really afraid of an accident?' cried Mrs Barnes. She held Gabriel's photograph closely.

'Of course not,' said Miss Flood-Porter. 'But we are a long way from home, and we don't speak the language.'

'We're all right in trains and hotels,' cut in Miss Rose. 'But we would feel lost if we missed our train in some small place.'

'What shall we do, Mr Barnes?' said the older sister. 'Shall we take my sister's dream as a warning? Shall we travel back tomorrow?'

'No *don't*,' said Iris to herself quietly.

She held her breath and waited for the vicar's reply. She did not want to travel on the same train as these people.

'You must do what you think is best,' said the vicar. 'But you will lose a day of your holiday if you go early.'

'Our tickets are for the day after tomorrow,' said Miss Rose. 'We don't want any difficulties. And now, I'm going to get my things ready for my journey back to dear old England.'

To everyone's surprise, she seemed to be almost crying. Miss Flood-Porter waited until her sister was gone from the sitting-room. Then she explained.

'We had a bad time, just before we came away. The doctor ordered a complete change. So we came here instead of Switzerland.'

Then the hotel manager came in and turned on the radio. He tried to get London for them. There was a lot of noise, then a well-known voice. 'You have just been listening to . . .'

But they heard nothing.

Miss Flood-Porter saw her garden, silver in the light of the full moon.

Miss Rose was putting her shoes in the bottom of a suitcase. Suddenly her hands shook. She remembered a terrible hole in a flowerbed, instead of the beautiful white flowers. . . . They never knew where the enemy would attack next. . . .

The vicar and his wife thought of their baby, asleep at home.

Iris remembered her friends on the noisy, racing train. Suddenly she wanted to be at home.

England was calling.

4

Iris was woken that night, as usual, by the sound of the fast train. She jumped out of bed and hurried to the window. She saw the train drawing a line of fire along the side of the lake. It raced below the hotel, and she could see the lighted windows.

She thought of it, speeding across the map. Names appeared

before her eyes and were gone – Bucharest, Zagreb, Trieste, Milan, Basle, Calais.

Once again she was filled with home-hunger. But she also remembered the mountains, and felt afraid.

Suppose . . . something . . . happens, and I never come back.

A railway crash, illness, or crime, were possible. These things happened to other people, all around her. Would the square mark on her hand keep her safe?

She lay awake. She was glad that this was the last night in this uncomfortable bed. For the next two nights she too would be racing through the dark.

The thought was with her when she woke the next morning. 'I'm going home today,' she told herself happily.

The air was cold when she looked out of her window. The lake shone greenly through the yellow leaves on the trees. But she did not care about the blue and gold beauty of autumn any more.

In her mind, Iris was already away from the hotel. Her journey was beginning before she started. She hardly noticed the other guests when she went down to the restaurant.

The Misses Flood-Porter were eating at a table by the window. They did not speak to her. Iris didn't notice. They were gone completely out of her life. She drank her coffee in silence. The sisters were talking about some people in England who were getting married. They hoped the weather would be good.

Her luck held. She did not have to speak to anyone At the desk, she saw a waiter giving Mrs Barnes a letter. That letter made a difference to Iris's future.

The vicar was outside, wearing holiday clothes. He smiled happily. 'What a good man he looks,' Iris thought.

'Is that a letter from home?' called the vicar.

'Yes,' answered his wife, after a short silence.

'I thought Grandma said she would not send any more letters. What is she writing about?'

'She wants me to do a little shopping for her, on our way through London.'

'But you'll be tired. It's not very kind of her.'

'No.' Mrs Barnes's voice was very sharp. 'It's *not*. Why didn't she *think*?'

Iris was glad that she did not have to worry about that sort of thing.

She walked past the front of the hotel. She kept away from the newly-married couple. They were having coffee and fruit in the open air.

Iris did not like the Todhunters. Their love, so beautiful and perfectly-dressed, made her feel sad.

The man looked into his wife's eyes with complete and close interest.

'Has it been perfect?' he asked.

Mrs Todhunter knew how long to wait before her answer. 'Yes.'

He understood what she did not say.

'Not perfect, then,' he said. 'But, darling, is anything . . .'

Iris moved away. She thought sadly of her own love. It was nothing but photographs in the newspapers.

The morning seemed endless. But at last it was over. Her suitcase was ready. The sun shone through the thick roof of leaves. But the iron chair was too hard and cold for comfort. The train was not coming for an hour. She decided to wait for it at the station.

The act of leaving the hotel brought her nearer to the journey. She enjoyed paying her bill. She hurried through the garden hoping not to meet anyone. She was afraid that she would be stopped at the last minute.

It was strange to be wearing fashionable clothes again. It was not very comfortable, but she welcomed it. It was part of the return to city life. She walked down the rough road. A man followed her, carrying her suitcase. She got to the station and sat down with her suitcase at her feet. The lake shone below her. She felt really happy.

There were other people at the station. Some just came to watch the fast train. They were happy and noisy, speaking many languages. Iris heard no English until two men came down the road from the village.

They were standing behind her, arguing. She was not interested enough to turn round. But their voices told her what they looked like.

The younger one had an excited voice. Iris felt sure he had a quick brain, with plenty of ideas. He spoke too quickly, sometimes getting the words wrong.

Iris began to like him. His mind was like hers. She did not like the other speaker. He spoke very slowly and carefully. He sounded like a clever man who never changed his mind.

'Oh no, my dear Hare,' said the older man. 'You are quite wrong. It is easy to know when someone is telling the truth. Some people always tell the truth, others don't. Look at that woman with the very red lips. What do you think of her?'

'Pretty.'

'Hum. What about the English lady in the raincoat? Suppose both those two told you something different. Which would you believe? They can't both be telling the truth.'

'I don't agree, Professor. Perhaps one of them tells me that a kind of flower is blue. The other says it's white. But that kind of flower can be either blue or white. So they're both right.'

'But supposing that one must be right, and the other must be wrong. Which one would you believe?'

Iris looked at the two women. One was a strongly-built Englishwoman with a good, kind face. The other was a pretty dark woman with red lips and large eyes, wearing a skin-tight skirt. She looked like a wild country woman who stole chickens for her supper.

Against her wishes, Iris agreed with the Professor. But she was angry with the younger man, because he stopped arguing.

'I see what you mean,' he said. 'The British raincoat wins every time . . . come and have a drink.'

'Thank you. Please let me order it. I like speaking the language.'

'You teach Modern Languages, don't you? Are there many girl students in your classes?'

'Yes – unluckily.'

Iris was sorry when they moved away. The crowd at the station got larger. The train was coming in twenty-five minutes, if it was on time. Other people were now sitting beside her. A child sat on her suitcase.

She did not mind. The sunshine, the green leaves, the lake, all gave her a feeling of quiet happiness.

There was nothing to warn her of the attack. She was hit without realizing it.

The back of her neck hurt suddenly. The white topped mountains turned over. The blue sky went black. She dropped down into darkness.

5

Iris's sight returned, at first, in bits and pieces. She saw parts of faces moving through the air. It seemed to be the same face, yellow-skinned, with black eyes and bad teeth.

She realized that she was lying on a seat in a dark room. A ring of women stood round her.

They looked down at her, half interested, like people looking at a dying animal in the street.

'Where am I?' she asked wildly.

A woman in a black dress suddenly began to speak in an unknown language. Iris felt the same fear of the day before in the mountains. The woman was so close that she could see the marks on her skin. But she was as impossible to understand as someone on the moon.

She wanted someone to tell her what was happening. I was glad to run away from the people at the hotel, she thought. But now I just want to see the strong, good face of the vicar looking down at me. Or the kind eyes of his wife.

She looked around her. She seemed to know the place. It had dark wooden walls. A line of sunlight shone from a high window.

She lifted her head higher. It made her feel sick. Then suddenly she remembered.

This was the waiting-room at the station. She was here yesterday, with the crowd. She remembered sitting outside in the sun, waiting for the train.

I was on my way back to England. But what happened then? Has the train come – and gone – and left me behind? she wondered.

Her head swam again. She tried to look at her watch. She discovered that she still had twenty-five minutes before the train came.

What happened to me? she wondered. Was I attacked?

She closed her eyes, and tried to clear her brain. Suddenly she remembered her bag. She put out her hand. It was not beside her. She could not see it anywhere on the seat. Her suitcase was on the floor, with her hat on top of it.

'My bag,' she cried, wild-eyed. 'Where's my bag?'

It held her money, her tickets, and her passport. She could not continue her journey without it.

The thought drove her mad. These women have stolen it, she thought. She tried to get up but they held her down. She fought against them. Her head hurt. There were strange sounds in her ears, and lights before her eyes.

The woman in the black dress held her. A fat girl held a glass to her lips. She lay back, helpless.

I must be ill, thought Iris. All the English people are going tomorrow. The hotel will close very soon. I shall be left here alone. I must get away, while there is still time.

She felt sure that she would be all right if she could get on the train. She would get to somewhere she knew. She thought of Basle on the milky-green Rhine. There were good hotels there, where English was spoken. She could be ill in comfort there.

She must catch the train. So she must find her bag. She realized that someone was trying to speak to her.

It was an old man in a dirty shirt with a broken, lined face. He kept taking off his hat. Then he pointed, first upwards, and then to her head.

All at once she understood his meaning. He was telling her that she had sunstroke.

She felt better. Now she knew what was the matter. The illness was no longer a mystery. She smiled at the man. He put his hand into his shirt and pulled out her bag.

With a cry, she took it from him. She opened it with shaking fingers. She was completely surprised. Tickets, money, passport – were still there.

Now at last she knew what to do. She gave them all money. The women accepted it without a word or smile. But the old man smiled happily, and picked up Iris's suitcase for her. She showed him her ticket.

The result was electric. He shouted excitedly. He took her arm and raced to the door with her. Now Iris understood the strange sounds.

The train was standing in the station. It was about to leave. The station was filled with action. Doors were being closed. People were shouting goodbye, and crowding in front of the carriages. There was a man holding up a flag.

They were one minute too late. Iris realized it. But the old man ran at the crowd like a tiger. There was still strength in his old body. He reached the nearest carriage and pulled open the door.

A grand old lady in black tried to stop him from entering. But he pushed past her and threw the suitcase in. Then he pulled Iris in after it.

The carriage was already moving when the old man jumped out. He was already yards behind when Iris turned to thank him. The station moved by. Then the lake passed the window, green and shining in the sun. Iris looked back for a last sight of the village. Now it was just a group of little coloured buildings on the side of the valley.

6

The train was speeding through a deep green valley, full of trees. Iris looked at her watch. It showed the same time as before.

It must have stopped when I crashed, she decided. It nearly made me lose the train.

She was very glad to be on her way back to England. More has happened to me in the last twenty-four hours, she thought, than in the rest of my life. I've been without friends, without money, sick, cut off from everything. And then, at the worst moment, my luck changed. It always does.

Iris usually travelled with magazines, chocolates, flowers and friends. This journey was different. The carriage was not very comfortable. She did not have much room. The train was not very clean. But she felt happy and excited.

The country was still very wild. The train made its way through great rocky valleys. They looked like a Doré picture of Dante's *Inferno*. Rivers raced down the mountain sides. Sometimes they passed dark lakes in lonely valleys.

Iris looked out through the window. She was glad that there was glass between her and the world outside. I've just met the real world for the first time, she thought.

She did not like to think of the railway station. Someone could easily have stolen my handbag, she thought. But the little old man saved me. I'm always lucky. But it must be terrible for some of the others.

She thought of all the unlucky people with no square marks on their hands. Supposing that there was a railway accident? She would always be in a safe part of the train. But other passengers would be in the crashed carriages.

She grew cold at the thought. She looked at the woman who sat in front of her in the carriage. She was not the kind of person you usually noticed at all. There was nothing interesting about her. She was middle-aged, unmarried, with short fair hair and a grey skin.

Usually Iris would not notice her. But today she looked at her kindly.

If *she* was in trouble, she thought, no one would help' her out.

There were plenty of people like that, without friends or money. No one would miss them. They could disappear without leaving any mark.

Iris looked at the other people in the carriage. There were six. On her side was a family – two large parents and one small daughter of about twelve.

The father had a round head, with no hair, and a fat neck. He wore thick glasses. His wife had straight black hair, combed flat. The girl wore children's shoes, but had a grown-up face.

They were all reading the same newspaper. The mother looked at the fashions. The little girl read the children's page. The father was studying the business news.

She looked away from them to the other side of the carriage. A fair, pretty girl was sitting next to the middle-aged lady. Clearly she wanted to look like a film actress. She had the same long fair hair and large blue eyes. Her face and lips were carefully painted.

But her beauty was without life. She wore a modern white suit, with a high black shirt. Her hat, gloves, and bag were also black. She sat very straight, without moving, as if she was being photographed.

She was sitting very close to the middle-aged lady. This left plenty of room for the person on her other side. It was the grand old lady in black.

This lady clearly belonged to an important family. Her eyes were cold and commanding. She was dressed in heavy black and filled almost half the seat.

She gave Iris a long angry look. Iris was surprised. It made her feel uncomfortable.

I know I pushed into the carriage, she thought. But *she's* got plenty of room. I wish I could explain.

She turned towards her and spoke.

'Do you speak English?'

Clearly the lady did not like the question. She closed her eyes, as if she did not want to look at Iris.

Iris bit her lip and looked at the other passengers. The family kept their eyes on their newspaper. The middle-aged lady looked down at her hands. The fair-haired beauty looked straight ahead.

They all seem to be afraid of her, thought Iris. Can't anyone speak until she does? Well, to *me*, she's nothing but a fat old woman.

She tried to hold onto this feeling. But an air of power seemed to come from the large black form.

Now she felt less excited. She remembered the sunstroke. Her head began to hurt again. This warned her to be careful.

I don't want to be ill, she thought. I mustn't tire myself by getting angry.

The carriage was getting very hot. The old lady in black seemed to make the air hotter and heavier. Iris looked towards the closed windows. She was sitting nearest to the train's corridor. But the corridor was crowded and hot. So she got to her feet and moved towards the window on the outside.

'Do you mind?' she asked. She hoped they would realize what she meant.

The man of the family got up and put his hand on the window. But instead of helping her to open it, he looked at the old lady in black. Then he shook his head at Iris.

Iris felt very angry. She returned to her corner.

I've got to accept it, she thought. I'm the stranger here.

This was another new feeling. She was used to being the most popular person in the crowd. Now she was a stranger to everyone.

Soon the door opened, and a tall man came into the carriage. I've never seen such a terrible face, thought Iris. He was very white, with dead dark eyes, and a short black beard.

He began to talk to the grand old lady. His story was clearly interesting. Iris noticed that the other passengers, even the child, listened carefully.

As he was speaking, his glasses shone round the carriage. At last he looked at Iris. He seemed surprised to see her, and not very pleased. ·

He put his lips close to the old lady's ear, and asked a question in a low voice. She replied very quietly.

Am I being stupid, wondered Iris. Or do these people really hate me? I'm beginning to think that everyone is my enemy. That really *is* stupid. The man with the black beard has never seen me before.

She shut her eyes, and tried to forget the people in the carriage. But the man's white face seemed to break through her closed eyes.

She was glad when his voice stopped, and she heard him go out of the carriage. She felt better at once. But her head was hurting again. The most important things in life were tea and cigarettes. But she dared not smoke, for fear of being sick. And tea seemed like an impossible dream.

The train was now racing through an empty country of rocks and trees. There were no houses. Sometimes they passed a very old castle. Then a man put his head in at the door, and shouted something.

The other passengers took no notice. But Iris began to open her bag, in case her ticket or passport was needed. Then, to her surprise, she heard an English voice.

The middle-aged lady was standing up and was asking her a question.

'Are you coming to the restaurant to get tea?'

7

Iris was too surprised to reply. She looked out of the window, to make sure that they were still in a strange country.

'Oh,' she cried, 'you're English.'

'Of course. I thought I looked English. . . . Are you coming to tea?'

'Oh *yes*.'

Iris followed her out of the carriage.

'It's a very long train,' the middle-aged lady said, 'because it's one of the last fast trains of the year. It's very full. It was difficult to get everyone in.'

She was the type of person who knows everything.

'Just look at the next carriage to ours as we go past – and I'll tell you something.'

Iris was not very interested, but she looked. Afterwards, she was sorry, because she could not forget what she saw.

A human form, covered with blankets, was lying along the seat. It was impossible to see if it was a man or a woman. The head and eyes and the whole face were bandaged. Clearly the face was terribly cut.

Iris stepped back. Then she saw who was looking after the sick person. It was the man with the white face and the black beard. Beside him was a nurse. But she did not look like a kind person. Her face was hard.

They were talking together. The sick person slowly lifted one hand, but they took no notice.

Iris felt very sorry. Supposing it was me, lying there? she thought.

'That nurse looks like a criminal,' she said in a low voice. 'It's terrible to be ill on a journey. And why don't they pull the curtain?'

'Perhaps they want to see out,' said the English lady.

'Poor thing. I suppose it's a man?'

She wanted the sick person to be as different as possible from herself.

'No, a woman,' said the English lady. 'They got in at our station. The doctor was telling the baroness about it. She's just been terribly hurt in a car accident. The doctor is taking her to the hospital in Trieste. They're trying to save her mind, and her life.'

'Is that man with the black beard a doctor?' asked Iris.

'Yes, very clever too.'

'Is he? I don't like him.' But the English lady did not hear her. They were pushing past people in the corridors. Then

27

they ran into a woman dressed in grey, standing at the door of a crowded carriage.

'Oh, I'm so sorry,' she said. 'I was just looking out to see if our tea was coming.'

Iris recognized Mrs Barnes's voice, and stepped back. She did not want to meet the vicar and his wife.

But Iris's new friend cried out, 'Oh, you're English too. This is my lucky day.' Mrs Barnes's soft brown eyes looked very friendly. So she added, 'I've been away for a year.'

'Are you on your way home?' asked Mrs Barnes warmly.

'Yes, but I can't believe it. It's much too good to be true. Shall I send a waiter with your tea?'

'That would be really kind. My husband is such a bad traveller. Like so many big strong men.'

Iris's head was beginning to hurt again. Now that Mrs Barnes was talking about her husband, they would never get past.

'Aren't we in the way?' she asked.

Mrs Barnes recognized her and tried to smile. She remembered about Gabriel's photograph.

'Are you surprised to see us?' she asked. 'We decided not to wait for the last fast train, after all. And our friends, the Miss Flood-Porters, came with us. In fact we're all here. The honeymoon couple are here too.'

They moved further down the corridor. The middle-aged lady turned to Iris. 'What a sweet face your friend has,' she said.

'Oh, she's not my friend,' answered Iris.

They reached the restaurant. It seemed full already. The Misses Flood-Porter – both wearing white travelling coats – were sitting at a table, drinking tea. They smiled at Iris, then quickly looked away.

We'll speak to you on the journey, they seemed to say. But in London we will become strangers.

The middle-aged lady found the last empty table, and sat down.

'I've ordered the tea for your nice friends,' she told Iris. 'Oh, isn't all this *fun*?'

Iris didn't really think so. She looked at the dirty tablecloth, and at the little plate of jam, full of bits of dirt. But the middle-aged lady looked so pleased that Iris smiled.

She did not look at her new friend closely. But she noticed the shining eyes, and the bright, excited voice, like a young girl's.

Later, Iris remembered the strange difference between the middle-aged face and the young voice. And it made everything seem like a dream.

The sun was shining in through the window. She held up one hand to keep the sun out of her eyes. She listened to the excited voice. She seemed to be talking to someone much younger than herself.

'Why do you like it?' she asked.

'Because it's travel. We're moving. Everything's moving.'

Iris tried to drink some tea before it was all shaken out of her cup. She learned that the lady was an English governess – Miss Winifred Froy. She was on her way home for a holiday. This adult lady still had living parents. It was a surprise to Iris.

'Mother and Father talk of nothing else but my return,' said Miss Froy. 'They're as excited as children. And so is Sock.'

'Sock?' repeated Iris.

'Yes, short for Socrates. Father's name for him. He's our dog. He's big and hairy, and he loves me so much. Mother says he understands that I'm coming home. But he doesn't know *when*. So the stupid old darling meets every train. Then he comes back with his tail down, looking so sad. He'll be wild with excitement the night I *do* come.'

Iris was not interested in the old parents. But she liked dogs. She got a clear picture of Sock, a big hairy dog, jumping about with excitement.

Suddenly Miss Froy remembered something.

'I'm sorry I didn't help you about the window. It *wa.* hot. But I didn't like to help, because of the baroness.'

'Do you mean the terrible black person?'

'Yes, the baroness,' said Miss Froy. 'She was kind about my seat in the train. I couldn't find my seat, so the baroness said I could travel in her carriage.'

29

'But she doesn't look kind,' said Iris quietly.

'She's very important. She belongs to the family to which I was governess. I must not mention names. But they were the very highest in the place. They're very powerful. Everyone does what they say.'

'That's bad,' said Iris.

'Yes it is, but you get used to it.'

'Are you going back again?'

'Yes, but not to the castle. I need another twelve months to learn the language perfectly. So I'm going back to teach the children of – well, they're the enemies of the other family.'

She lowered her voice.

'There is a small group of people who hate the man I used to work for. They say all kinds of bad things about him. I don't know if they're true. It's not my business. I only know that he's a wonderful man. . . . Shall I tell you a secret?'

Iris was beginning to feel tired of Miss Froy.

'I wanted to say "goodbye" to him,' continued Miss Froy. 'I hoped he was not angry because I was going to work for his enemy. Everyone told me that he was away at his country house. But I didn't believe them. I lay awake until the early morning. Then I heard water splashing about in the bathroom . . . there is only one bathroom, the castle was so old-fashioned. So I went out very quietly, and met him in the corridor. There we were, just a man and woman, both in our night clothes. His hair was all wet and rough. But he was wonderful. He shook my hand, and thanked me for everything.'

Miss Froy finished her tea.

'I'm so glad to be friendly with everyone. Of course I'm not important. But I can truly say that I haven't got an enemy in the world.'

8

'And now,' said Miss Froy, 'we had better go back to the baroness's carriage. That will make room for others.'

Iris followed Miss Froy down the shaking restaurant carriage. The Misses Flood-Porter took no notice of her, but they looked hard at Miss Froy. Miss Froy looked back at them.

'Those people are English,' she said quietly to Iris. She did not know that Iris already knew them.

They made their long and shaky journey down the train. Miss Froy seemed very happy. She laughed aloud when she nearly fell over.

She looked into the carriages as they went past. 'Do look,' she said once. 'There's a beautiful couple, just like film actors.'

Iris felt too tired to be interested. But she looked quickly through the glass. She saw the honeymoon couple from the hotel. The wife was wearing very beautiful clothes. All kinds of expensive things were lying about in the carriage.

'Oh look,' said Miss Froy. 'They've got all that expensive fruit with their tea. He's looking at her with his heart in his eyes. But I can't see her face. Oh, lady, please turn your head.'

Her wish came true. At that moment Mrs Todhunter turned towards the window. She saw Miss Froy and spoke to her husband. He got up at once, and pulled the curtain.

Iris felt angry, but Miss Froy only laughed.

'He'll remember me,' Miss Froy said. 'He looked at me as if he'd like to kill me. But I understand. I was the World. And he wants to forget the World. It must be wonderful to be so much in love.'

They reached the end of the corridor. Iris could not help looking into the sick woman's carriage. She saw the human form and a face covered in bandages. Then she looked away quickly, before her eyes met the eyes of the doctor.

His eyes frightened her. They seemed to have a strange power. Usually she did not notice that kind of thing. But she was very tired, and her head hurt. Everything seemed unreal. She was in a kind of dream. It was partly because of the sun-stroke.

Outside their carriage, Miss Froy turned to her.

'I won't sit silent any more. I'm not afraid of the baroness. We're *English*.'

They sat down. Iris felt braver too. She had a cigarette.

'Have you travelled much?' she asked Miss Froy.

'Only in Europe. My mother doesn't really like me going so far from home. So I've promised not to go further than Europe.'

'Is your mother very old?'

'No, she's eighty years young. Father is seventy-seven. He never let her know that he was younger than she. But she found out when he had to stop work at sixty-five. Oh, I can't believe that I'm really going to see them again soon.'

Iris tried to listen, but she got very tired of the family story.

'I'm sure you have had a wonderful life,' she said, after a while.

'Had, and still have,' said Miss Froy. 'Lots of young men have asked me to marry them. It's because of my fair hair. And I still have hopes. I never forget that a little boy is born for every little girl. And even if we haven't met yet, I'm sure we *shall*.'

Iris wanted to be quiet, but Miss Froy's voice went on and on.

But then Iris became more interested. Miss Froy was talking about languages. 'I speak ten, including English,' she said. 'At first you can't understand a word, when you're in a strange country. But by the end of a year you can speak the language really well.'

'*I* always hope the other people can speak English,' said Iris.

'But sometimes they can't,' said Miss Froy. 'Then you can be in terrible trouble. Shall I tell you a true story?'

At once she began a story which made Iris feel even worse.

'A certain woman was found to be mad. They came to take her away. But by mistake they went to the wrong house, and took away an Englishwoman. She couldn't speak a word of the language. She didn't know what was happening. She was so afraid that she acted as if she really was mad. So they kept her quiet with drugs.

'Then the doctor discovered his mistake. But he did not dare tell anyone. At last a nurse saved her, and she was set free. But what a terrible thing for that poor Englishwoman. She was alone, in a strange place. She couldn't understand a word. Can you imagine . . .'

'Please *stop*,' broke in Iris. 'I can imagine it all. Very clearly. But do you mind if we stop talking.'

'Oh certainly. Aren't you well?'

'I've got a bit of a headache. I've just had sunstroke.'

'Sunstroke? When?'

Iris told her about the attack. She looked round the carriage. The other passengers clearly didn't understand English. Except for the baroness. Did she understand? She had a stupid face, but she seemed to be listening to them.

'Oh, you poor thing,' cried Miss Froy. 'Why didn't you stop me talking before? Let me give you something.'

She looked in her handbag.

'These will make you feel better. Take them, then try to get a little sleep.'

Iris closed her eyes. She knew Miss Froy was still watching her kindly. It made her feel safe. The carriage was very warm. She was feeling sleepy. On and on went the train. Clankety-clankety-*clank*.

The drug began to work. Her head kept falling forwards. Soon she forgot where she was. She seemed to be moving through the air. She could hear the noise of the train wheels. Clankety-clankety-*clank*. She was moving higher and higher The carriage was like an aeroplane. Then she was falling down and down.

She opened her eyes with a jump. She could hear her heart. She wondered where she was. Then she recognized the carriage. She was looking at the baroness.

She looked away to the seat in front of her.

To her surprise, Miss Froy's place was empty.

9

Iris was glad that Miss Froy was gone. She didn't want to hear any more about her family for a while. She wanted to be quiet.

No one else in the carriage took any notice of her. The baroness was asleep in her corner.

Probably Miss Froy has gone to wash, she thought. I hope she doesn't come back yet. Every time someone passed she thought it was Miss Froy. But Miss Froy didn't come. Iris was glad. No more talk about Father and Mother. Or even Sock.

She could hear the noise of the wheels on the rails. Clankety-clankety-*clank*. It sounded almost like the sea, racing over the rocks. Clankety-clankety-*clank*.

Suddenly Iris woke up again. The baroness was asleep. But for a moment Iris felt afraid. She looked at Miss Froy's place.

It was still empty.

This time Iris was sorry that she wasn't there. A while ago she was glad to be without her. But now she felt lonely.

Probably I'll soon be wishing she'd go away again, she said to herself. But she is human.

She looked at the fair-haired beauty. There seemed to be no life in her. She was like something in a shop window.

But Miss Froy was so full of life. Iris looked at her watch. It was getting late. She began to be worried.

She's had enough time to take a bath, she thought. I – I hope there's nothing wrong.

She tried to forget the idea.

How stupid, she told herself. What *could* happen to her? It's not night. So she hasn't opened the wrong door by mistake, and stepped out of the train in the dark. She's used to travelling, too. And she speaks about a hundred languages.

This gave her another idea.

Yes, she's a great talker. She's probably talking to someone.

She's very friendly, and she wants to tell everyone that she's going home. I'll wait another half an hour.

She looked out of the window. The clouded sky of late afternoon had a sad look. They were out of the mountains now, and travelling through flat green country. It was an autumn picture. Summer is over, she thought.

The time passed too quickly. Iris did not know what she would do at the end of the half-hour.

Then the other passengers began to move. The little girl was asking about something. She's tired, thought Iris. She probably wants to go to sleep.

The mother took off the little girl's shoes. Then she pointed to Miss Froy's empty place.

Iris did not like to see the little girl sitting in Miss Froy's corner.

What will Miss Froy say when she comes back? she wondered.

The little girl was so heavy with sleep that she closed her eyes at once. The parents looked at each other and smiled. They looked at the fair-haired beauty, and she smiled as well.

I wish they wouldn't take Miss Froy's place, thought Iris. They must realize that she's coming back. Or do they know something that I don't know? Perhaps they know she *isn't* coming back.

Iris looked quickly at her watch. The half-hour was over.

Outside the window the grey sky was getting darker. It made her feel sad. She wanted to hear happy voices, lights, laughing. And she wanted to see a little, lined middle-aged face, and hear the high, excited voice.

Now that she was gone, she seemed like a dream. Iris did not have a clear picture of her in her mind.

What was she *like*? she wondered.

Then she looked up. To her surprise, Miss Froy's suitcase was no longer there.

She tried not to worry. But she was beginning to feel afraid. Has she moved to another carriage? she thought. But no, there are no empty seats. She told me that herself. I'm sure she wouldn't leave me without saying anything. And she paid for

35

my tea. I must give her the money back. So I must find her.

She looked at the other passengers. She didn't care what they thought of her. She must try to speak to them. She started in German.

'Wo ist die dame *English*?'

They shook their heads to show that they did not understand. She tried again.

'Où est la dame *English*?'

There was no sign of understanding on their faces. She tried in her own language.

'Where is the English lady?'

It was useless. She could not reach them. They looked at her coldly.

She pointed at Miss Froy's seat, and gave them a questioning look. The man and his wife smiled at each other. The fair-haired girl looked away. The little girl opened her black eyes and began to laugh. Her father gave her a warning look, and she stopped.

Iris suddenly felt angry. She got up and went over to the baroness. She shook her arm.

'Wake up, please,' she said.

The other passengers looked worried. They seemed afraid of the baroness. But Iris took no notice. The baroness opened her eyes and looked at her coldly.

'Where is Miss Froy?' asked Iris.

'Miss Froy?' repeated the baroness. 'I do not know anyone who has that name.'

Iris pointed to the seat where the little girl was sitting.

'She sat *there*,' she said.

The baroness shook her head.

'You are making a mistake,' she said. 'No English lady has ever sat there.'

Iris couldn't understand it.

'But she *did*,' she cried. 'I talked to her. And we went and had tea together. You must remember.'

'There is nothing to remember.' The baroness spoke slowly. 'I do not understand what you mean at all. There has been no English lady in this carriage at any time, except you. You are the only English lady here.'

Iris opened her lips, but closed them again. She had a helpless feeling. She could not believe what the baroness said. But the baroness was a commanding person of great power.

She looked straight into the girl's eyes. Iris looked at the heavy face. Deep lines ran downwards from the mouth to the chin. The lips were turned down at the corners.

Iris did not say any more. She realized that the baroness would not listen. She would just repeat that Miss Froy was never there.

Iris sat down. Her brain was going round and round. She hardly noticed the country moving past the window, or the other passengers. It was getting dark. A village suddenly appeared in the shadows, then disappeared again. She could see the dark roofs, and a little river racing under a bridge.

The next second, the church and the wooden houses were left behind. The fast train hurried on towards England.

No Miss Froy? thought Iris. The woman must be mad. Does she think I'm a fool? . . . But why does she say it? *Why*?

This was what worried her most. Miss Froy never hurt anyone. She had no enemies. She was friendly with everyone.

But she was gone. Iris was sure now that she would not come back to the carriage. Suddenly she jumped up.

She must be somewhere on the train, she said to herself. I'll find her.

Iris could not think why Miss Froy left her. Does she think I'm ill? she thought. And is she afraid she'll catch the illness? After all, she wants to get back to the old parents and the dog.

It was hard work getting down the train. Last time Miss Froy was in front, remembered Iris. She cleared a way for me. But now there were more passengers standing in the corridors.

Iris did not know how to ask them to move. She did not like to push. The men noticed her because she was pretty.

Whenever she fell against one of them, they thought she was trying to be friendly.

She was getting hot and tired. She felt ill. She looked into each carriage, but all the faces looked the same. They were like something in a dream.

She was glad to see the vicar and his wife in one of the crowded carriages.

They were sitting facing each other. Mr Barnes's eyes were closed. His face was white. He did not look at all well.

His wife watched him. She looked unhappy. She imagined all his feelings of train-sickness.

She did not smile when Iris went in and spoke to her.

'I'm sorry to trouble you, but I'm looking for my friend.'

'Oh yes?'

Mrs Barnes tried to sound bright. But her eyes were unhappy.

'You remember her,' said Iris. 'She sent the waiter with your tea.'

The vicar came to life.

'It was very kind,' he said. 'Will you give her my thanks?'

'I will, when I find her,' promised Iris. 'She went out of the carriage some time ago . . . and she hasn't come back.'

'I haven't noticed her pass the window,' said Mrs Barnes. 'Perhaps she went to wash. She can't possibly be lost.'

'Can I find her for you?' asked the vicar, getting bravely to his feet.

'Certainly *not*.' His wife's voice was sharp. 'Don't be stupid, Kenneth. You don't know what she looks like.'

The vicar sat down again, and smiled at Iris.

'Isn't it terrible to be such a bad traveller?' he said.

'Try not to talk,' said his wife.

Iris went out of the carriage. The vicar's illness was very unlucky. She knew that he was good and kind, and also strong and clever. But he could not help her because he was ill.

She got more and more worried. I *must* find her, she thought. I'm the only person on the whole train who cares about a missing passenger.

She went past the Todhunters' window. The curtain was

still drawn. She recognized the Misses Flood-Porter in the next carriage. The older lady wore glasses, and was reading a book. Miss Rose was smoking a cigarette. They looked very comfortable. They were kind-hearted. But they were glad to be sitting down, while others had to stand.

At last she got to the restaurant. Tea was finished, and it was full of men drinking and smoking.

She looked around the carriage. She saw the black-bearded doctor through the smoke. His face was white and bony. His dead eyes looked bigger behind his thick glasses.

He was looking at her coldly. Suddenly – for no reason at all – she thought of the doctor in Miss Froy's terrible story.

II

Iris knew that everyone was looking at her. But she didn't care.

'Please,' she called out in a loud voice, 'Is there anyone English here?'

The sight of a pretty girl in trouble made a young man jump to his feet.

'Can I be of use?' he asked quickly.

Iris knew his voice. She remembered it from the railway station, just before her sunstroke. He's the young man who was arguing with the professor, she realized. The young man had a piece of hair which stood up on his head. It was the kind of hair which lies down when brushed, but jumps up again at once. She liked the look of him. But was he too young to help?

Iris found that her voice was shaking. She could not think clearly. She tried to explain.

'It's all rather difficult,' she said. 'I'm in trouble. But it's nothing to do with me. I'm sure there's some mistake, and I can't speak a word of this terrible language.'

'That's all right,' said the young man brightly. 'I speak the language. Just tell me the trouble.'

39

Iris waited for a moment. A tall thin man got slowly to his feet. As soon as he spoke, Iris recognized the voice of the Professor of Modern Languages.

'May I help? I can speak the language,' he said coldly.

'He's no good,' broke in the young man. 'He only knows the rules of the language. I can say rude things in it. And we may need someone to be rude.'

Iris laughed. Then she stopped. She realized she was getting too excited.

'An Englishwoman has disappeared from the train,' she told the professor. 'She's a *real* person, but the baroness says . . .'

She stopped talking. She saw the doctor looking at her hard. The professor also looked at her with a cold eye.

'You will have to speak more slowly and clearly,' said the Professor.

She tried again. This time she told the story in a few words. She was careful not to mention the baroness.

The professor listened carefully.

'You said – an *English* lady?' he asked.

'Yes,' answered Iris. 'Miss Froy. She's a governess.'

'Ah yes. . . . Now are you quite certain that she is nowhere on the train?'

'Yes, I've looked everywhere.'

'Exactly when did she leave the carriage?'

'I don't know. I was asleep. When I woke up, she wasn't there.'

'Then we must first ask the other passengers.'

'Will you come with us?' Iris asked the young man. He probably speaks the language better than the professor, she thought.

Iris felt happier as they went back along the train. She was still worried about Miss Froy. But the young man made her feel better.

'My name's Hare,' said the young man. 'But you'd better call me Maximilian – or Max, if you prefer it. What's your name?'

'Iris Carr.'

'Mrs?'

'Miss.'

'Good. I work out here. I'm building a bridge up in the mountains.'

'What fun. I do nothing.'

Iris was feeling much better when they entered the baroness's carriage. She noticed at once that the black-bearded doctor was seated next to the baroness. He was talking to her in a quick voice. He must have left the restaurant in a hurry.

Iris smiled at the baroness.

'Two English gentlemen have come to ask about Miss Froy,' she said.

The baroness lifted her head and looked at her coldly. Iris could not tell what she was thinking.

'Will you kindly let me in?' asked the Professor.

Iris went out into the corridor. She could see the sick woman's carriage. The nurse looked different now. She didn't look like a criminal. She just looked stupid. Iris was worried. Perhaps I'm making mistakes about everything, she thought.

But then the first nurse, with the hard face, appeared at the door.

Iris smiled when Hare spoke to her.

'I'm going to listen to them,' he told her.

Iris tried to see what was happening.

The professor spoke first to the baroness, then to each person in the carriage.

Iris put her hand on Hare's arm.

'Is he learning anything about Miss Froy?' she asked.

He looked at her without smiling.

'It's all rather difficult,' he told her.

Her happiness began to cloud. The baroness was looking at her as she spoke to the professor. The professor listened carefully. Then she made a sign to the doctor.

The doctor's white face and dead eyes made him look like a dead man. But he began to talk and grew more and more lively. He moved his hands as he spoke.

The doctor finished speaking, and the professor turned to Iris.

'You have made a strange mistake,' he said. 'No one in this carriage knows anything about the lady.'

Iris looked at him. She could not believe it.

'Are you telling me that I imagined her?' she asked angrily.

'I don't know what to think.'

'Then I'll tell you,' said Iris. 'These people are not telling the truth.'

The professor grew colder.

'These people are all known to the baroness,' he said. 'The gentleman is the baroness's bank manager. He is well-known in this part of the country. The young lady is the daughter of a man who works for the baroness.'

'I don't know anything about that,' said Iris. 'But Miss Froy paid for my tea. I must give her back the money.'

'If you had tea together,' said the professor, 'the waiter will remember it. I will speak to him next. Please describe the lady to me.'

Iris was worried. 'I never looked closely at Miss Froy,' she said. 'The sun was in my eyes when we had tea. And later I kept my eyes closed because of my headache.' Iris realized she could not remember Miss Froy very well at all.

'I can't tell you very much,' she said slowly. 'She's middle-aged, rather colourless. She looks just like everyone else.'

'Tall or short? Fat or thin? Fair or dark?' asked Hare.

'She said she had fair hair.'

'Didn't you notice it yourself?'

'No. But I think it was a light colour. And I remember she had blue eyes.'

'Not very helpful,' said the professor.

'What did she wear?' asked Hare suddenly.

Iris was able to describe Miss Froy's clothes exactly. 'She wore a brown suit and a blue hat.'

'Are you sure you can't remember the face under the hat?' asked Hare.

'No, I can't. My head was hurting so much.'

'Exactly,' said the professor. 'The doctor has told us that you had sunstroke.'

At this moment the doctor started to speak to Iris himself.

'The sunstroke explains everything,' said the doctor in slow, careful English. 'You were ill. You saw someone who was not there. Then you went to sleep. You woke up and felt much better. So you saw Miss Froy no more. . . . She is nothing but a dream.'

12

At first Iris was too surprised to say anything. Hare and the professor looked at each other.

'That is the end of the problem,' said the professor. 'I hope you will soon feel better.'

'We'll go away and let Miss Carr get some rest,' said Hare, with a half-smile.

Iris tried not to sound angry.

'It's not as easy as that. It's not the end of the problem. What makes you think that I'm not telling the truth?'

'I do not,' said the professor. 'I think you have made a mistake. Can you explain why six persons did not tell the truth?'

Iris had a sudden idea.

'Probably one person began it,' she said. 'Then the others helped her. So it's her word against mine. But I'm English, and you're English, and Miss Froy's English. So you ought to believe *me*.'

'But *why* should the baroness not tell the truth? What reason has she?'

'I don't know,' said Iris weakly. 'It's all such a mystery. Miss Froy said she had no enemies. And she told me that the baroness was kind to her.'

'What have I done?' asked the baroness.

'She said that you let her sit in your carriage.'

'How kind of me. Unluckily I know nothing about it. And everyone here agrees with me.'

'I think she owns them all,' said Iris angrily. 'They all work for her.'

Hare spoke to the little girl. She did not want to move, but at last she got up and sat with her parents. Hare sat down in Miss Froy's seat.

'Don't worry,' he said to Iris. 'Other people on the train have probably seen Miss Froy.'

'I know,' agreed Iris. 'But I can't think. My brain's too tired.'

'If you think of anything more,' said the professor, 'please let me know. But I hope you will not make fools of us all again.'

He left the carriage.

'I hate that man,' cried Iris.

'Oh no,' said Hare. 'He's not bad. He's just afraid of you because you're young and pretty.'

Then he stopped smiling.

'I want to tell you a true story,' he said. 'Some years ago I played in an important football game at Twickenham. Before the game the Prince of Wales came and shook hands with both the teams. I was hit on the head during the game, and was taken to hospital. Later on, a nurse came in and said there was an important visitor to see me.'

'The Prince?' asked Iris, trying to sound interested.

'Yes. He only stayed for a few minutes. He just smiled at me and said he was sorry about my accident. The next morning the nurses said, "Were you pleased to see your captain?" '

'Captain?'

'Yes, the captain of the team. It wasn't the Prince. But I saw him as clearly as I see you. He was *real*. That's what a bit of head trouble can do to you.'

Iris closed her lips angrily.

'I thought you believed me,' she said. 'But you're like the rest. Please go away.'

'I will, because I'm sure you ought to keep quiet. Try and get some sleep.'

'No. I've got to think this out. I don't believe all of you and I'm not going mad. I'm not. I'm *not*.'

Hare decided to leave Iris alone and he went away. Iris sat in her corner, shaken by the fast-moving train. It was very noisy. She felt tired and hungry.

She jumped when a nurse appeared at the door. She called the doctor away. Iris hardly noticed. Her thoughts raced round in a circle.

I was on the platform one second . . . and the next second I went out, she thought. Where did I go? Was I really in the waiting-room? And all those women, and the funny old man. Were they *real*? Of course they were, because I'm on the train. . . . But I met Miss Froy *afterwards*. They say that she's only my dream. So that means that I have dreamed the waiting-room, and the train. I'm not on the train at all. I'm not awake yet. That can't be true. It's driving me mad.

She tried to think quietly.

I *am* awake, and I'm here on this train. So I *did* meet Miss Froy. . . . But there's some mystery. I must fight the people who aren't telling the truth. I *will*.

Suddenly everything became clear.

She jumped up from the seat. The baroness looked at her. 'Is madame worse?' she asked.

'Better, thanks,' answered Iris. 'I'm going to speak to some English visitors from my hotel. They saw me with Miss Froy.'

13

What has happened to Miss Froy? wondered Iris. I've searched the whole train. The corridors and carriages are full of tourists. She couldn't open a window or a door and jump out. People would notice that. And there's nowhere for her to hide.

Iris stopped worrying about it.

My job is to prove that she was really there, she thought. Other people must find her.

She opened her handbag and took out her pocket mirror.

The baroness watched her. Her face did not move. But her brain seemed to be working fast.

She's setting her brain against mine, thought Iris, suddenly hurrying. I must get there first.

As soon as she started to hurry, her hand shook. She painted a thick red mark round her mouth. She tired to find her comb, but couldn't. So she went out into the corridor.

Men looked at her, and women spoke angrily, as she pushed past them. She took no notice. In her mind she could almost see the little middle-aged lady somewhere ahead of her.

I must hurry to reach her, she thought. But faces kept coming in between her and Miss Froy. She pushed past them. Her face burned and her hair fell over her face.

At last she got to a clearer place in the corridor. She saw the professor. He was smoking and looking out of the window.

She slowed down. She was out of breath.

'Do I look terrible?' she asked him. 'It was that crowd of people. They wouldn't let me past.'

The professor did not smile. He did not like the look of her wild hair and bright colour. Mr Todhunter did not like the look of her either. He watched her through the open door of his compartment.

He liked pretty women. But he preferred a quiet lake to a racing river. He remembered Iris in her holiday clothes at the hotel. But he took no notice of her until she wore a pretty dress in the evening.

'Who's the girl?' asked his wife. She turned over the pages of a picture paper.

He lowered his voice.

'One of the crowd from the hotel.'

'Oh.'

In the next compartment Miss Flood-Porter lifted her head. Her sister woke and listened too.

Iris did not know that others were listening. She spoke to the professor in a high, excited voice.

'I can prove that Miss Froy was with me. The English visitors from my hotel saw her too. We'll get the police to stop the train at Trieste and search it.'

Iris was excited. She imagined the British flag flying over their heads.

The professor smiled in a tired way.

'I'm waiting to hear more,' he said.

'You *will* hear more,' answered Iris. She turned to Mr Todhunter. 'You'll help me find Miss Froy, won't you?' she asked brightly.

He smiled down at her, but did not answer at once.

'I shall be happy to help,' he told her. 'But . . . who *is* Miss Froy?'

'She's an English governess. She's missing from the train. Surely you remember her? She looked in at your window. You jumped up and closed the curtain.'

'I would have done that, yes,' said Todhunter. 'But it never happened. No lady looked through my window.'

Iris felt as if she was falling through space.

'You didn't *see* her?' she cried.

'No.'

'But your wife showed her to you. You were both angry.'

The beautiful Mrs Todhunter broke in.

'No one looked in. . . . Do you mind if we shut the door? I want to rest before dinner.'

The professor turned to Iris.

'You're tired,' he said. 'Let me take you back to your carriage.'

'No.' Iris shook off his hand. 'There are other people.'

She hurried into the next carriage. The Misses Flood-Porter were sitting up very straight.

'You'll help me find Miss Froy, won't you?' she said to them. 'She's *English*.'

The sisters both looked at her. Then Miss Rose spoke. 'I do not remember your friend,' she said. 'Perhaps you did have someone with you. But I was not wearing my glasses.'

'Neither was I,' said Miss Flood-Porter. 'So we shall not be able to help you.'

Iris could hardly believe her ears.

'But surely you'll help an Englishwoman in danger?' she asked hotly.

'Danger?' said Miss Rose. 'Nothing can happen to her on a crowded train. Other people have probably seen her. So don't ask *us* about her.'

Iris could not speak. The British flag was lying on the ground.

She hated them all. The vicar's wife came in. Iris looked at her silently.

'My husband is sleeping now,' she said with a smile. 'So I've come to talk to you all.'

Iris was just going out.

'Don't go away,' said Mrs Barnes.

'Nothing could keep me here.' Iris spoke in an angry, hopeless voice. 'I don't suppose *you* saw Miss Froy?'

'Was that the little lady in the brown suit, with the blue hat?' asked Mrs Barnes. 'Why, *of course* I remember her. She was so kind about the tea.'

14

Iris was almost in tears. She turned to the professor.

'Do you believe me now?' she asked in a shaky voice.

The professor looked at the vicar's wife. He liked that kind of woman. She was safely married to someone else.

'Your question is not necessary,' he said. 'I'm sorry I did not believe you before. It was because of your sunstroke.'

'Well, what are you going to do?' asked Iris.

The professor did not want to make any more mistakes.

'I think I'll go and speak to Hare,' he said. 'He speaks the language well, and he has a good brain.'

Iris was in a hurry but she stopped to speak to the vicar's wife.

'Thank you so very much.'

'I'm glad. But why are you thanking me?' asked Mrs Barnes, in surprise.

They found Hare in the restaurant. He was very surprised.

'I never really believed in Miss Froy,' he cried. 'But what's happened to her?'

The professor took off his glasses to clean them. His eyes looked weak, not cold. Iris felt quite friendly towards him now.

'The Misses Flood-Porter want to keep out of it,' she said. 'But why did those six people in the carriage say that she was not there?'

'Perhaps they didn't understand me,' said the professor.

'Yes they did,' broke in Hare. 'You spoke very well, professor.'

'I must think more about it,' said the professor.

'He means that he wants to smoke,' explained Hare. 'All right, professor. I'll take care of Miss Carr.'

They sat down at a table.

'Is Miss Froy really a stranger to you?' he asked.

'Of course.'

'But you're nearly going mad about her. You're a very kind person.'

'No I'm *not*,' said Iris. 'Usually I don't care about people. It's strange. I can't understand myself. She was very nice to me. Then she disappeared. And everyone said I imagined her. It was like a terrible dream.'

'But didn't you think it was because of your sunstroke?'

'No. Your story about being hit on the head was different. You saw a real person and thought that he was the Prince. But I was supposed to have talked to someone who wasn't there at all.'

She smiled with happiness as she looked out of the window.

They were going slowly through a small town. There were stony streets and poor-looking shops. The houses were built on the hillside. The grey paint was washed off them by the rain. They were a dirty white. Everything looked poor.

'What a terrible place,' said Iris. 'When do we reach Trieste?'

'Twenty minutes to ten.'

'It's five to six now. We must find her soon. Her old parents are waiting for her at home. The stupid old dog meets every train.'

She stopped – she realized that tears were appearing in her eyes. The crowd would laugh at this, she thought.

'I'll get you a drink,' said Hare.

'Don't go now,' she said, holding him back. 'There's that terrible doctor.'

The black bearded man seemed to be searching for someone. He came over to them.

'Your friend has returned to the carriage,' he said.

'Miss Froy?' cried Iris. 'How wonderful. Where was she?'

'All the time she was so near. She was talking to my nurses in the next carriage.'

'I never looked there,' said Iris, laughing.

'But why was there all that mystery?' asked Hare.

'We did not understand madame. She talked of an English lady. But this lady is German, or perhaps Austrian. She is not English.'

'I made that mistake too,' Iris told Hare. 'I didn't know she was English at first. She speaks every language. Come on. Let's go and see her.'

They passed the Barnes's carriage. The vicar was trying to be brave. His wife looked tired, with black circles under her eyes.

'Are you still looking for your friend?' she asked.

'No,' called Iris. 'She's found.'

They got to the professor's carriage.

'I want you to come too, and meet my Miss Froy,' she said. The professor followed her down the corridor.

'There she is,' she cried. 'There she is at the end of the corridor.'

She saw the well-known shape in the brown suit.

'Miss Froy,' she cried.

The lady turned. Iris saw her face. She stepped back with a cry.

'That's *not* Miss Froy,' she said.

15

Iris looked into the face of a stranger. She was thrown back into the darkness again, just when she thought she could see daylight. She felt that she was caught in a terrible dream. She fought to get free.

Miss Froy. She must hold on to Miss Froy. Suddenly she remembered her face quite clearly. It was old and young at the same time, with round blue eyes.

Someone else stood before her, wearingMiss Froy's brown suit. The face under the well-known hat was yellowish. The eyes were black.

'You are *not* Miss Froy,' cried Iris.

'No,' replied the woman in English. 'I am Frau Kummer. I told you my name when we had tea together.'

'That's not true. I never had tea with you. You're a stranger to me.'

'A stranger, certainly, but we talked together. We only talked a little, because your poor head was hurting.'

'*Ah*,' cried the doctor. Iris felt afraid.

'I mustn't let them frighten me,' she thought.

'This is *not* Miss Froy,' she said to the professor. 'But she's wearing her clothes.' She tried to stop her voice from shaking. 'Why? *Why*? What's happened to Miss Froy? . . . She says we had tea together, but we didn't. The waiter knows. Bring him.'

But Hare did not hurry off. Instead he stood and bit his lip.

'Why not give up and get some rest?' he said in a kind voice. It made Iris angry.

No one believed her. The darkness was closing around her again. Then she remembered the vicar's wife.

'Mrs Barnes,' she said weakly.

'I'll get her,' said the professor. He wanted to end the matter. He was a kind-hearted and fair man. But he didn't like young girls like Iris. He remembered well the unhappy end to his last term. One of his best students – a girl, suddenly acted very strangely. She came to his room to say goodbye. Then she began to cry. She said that she worked hard only to please him. She did not want to leave him. Unluckily the door was open. Everyone heard what she said. So now the professor did not want to meet any more excited girls.

He saw Mrs Barnes sitting with the Misses Flood-Porter.

'I'm sorry to trouble you,' he said. 'But would you mind coming to help us?'

'Certainly,' said Edna Barnes.

'You look very white,' said the professor, looking at her tired brown eyes. 'Not ill, I hope?'

'Oh no,' said Mrs Barnes, trying to sound bright.

'I don't like to worry you,' he said. 'The girl is very excited. She says now that the lady is not the same as the lady she first saw.'

'Let's hope it *is* the right one,' said Miss Flood-Porter quietly. 'If not, they'll stop the train at Trieste. Then we shall miss the train to Milan.'

They met the vicar in the corridor. He was searching for his wife.

'There you are, Ken,' cried Mrs Barnes.

Iris was sitting waiting for Hare to come back with the waiter. She had no real hope. She felt that the baroness had some strange power over all the people on the train.

Hare returned. 'You said the waiter had fair hair,' he said. 'This is the only one with fair hair. He speaks English.'

'Do you remember bringing my tea? Do you remember faces easily?'

'Certainly madame,' said the waiter.

'Please look at this lady. Don't look at her clothes, but look at her face. Now – is that the lady who was having tea with me?'

The waiter was silent for a moment.

'Yes madame,' he said at last.

'You're *sure*?'

'Yes madame. I am sure.'

Iris said nothing.

Suddenly there was a cry from the next carriage. The doctor jumped up at once. He hurried back to the sick person.

The cry did not seem human but strangely animal and full of fear with its 'M-m-m-m' sound. Iris remembered the poor broken body bandaged in the next compartment.

Then she heard the professor's voice coming down the train corridor.

'Mrs Barnes was the only one who remembered Miss Froy,' she said to Hare. 'I know she always tells the truth.'

Edna Barnes came in, holding her husband's arm. The vicar looked down at his wife.

'Edna, my dear,' he asked. 'Is this the lady?'

Mrs Barnes did not wait at all.

'Yes,' she said.

Iris heard a sound like wings inside her head. She fell down into the darkness.

16

Iris found herself sitting down. Someone was holding her head down.

'I'm quite all right now,' she said. She felt much better.

'Would you like to lie down?' asked Mr Barnes.

Iris needed a quiet place. She wanted to think about everything clearly.

'I want to talk to you,' she said to Hare.

He was very pleased. 'Come along to my carriage,' he said.

They went down the corridor, arm in arm. Iris noticed that the lights were on now. It was night. It was quite black outside the windows. But a few lights showed that they were reaching a town.

The train seemed hotter and smokier.

'Open the window wide,' cried Iris.

'There's plenty of air coming in at the top,' said Hare. But he opened the window.

'Do you remember talking to the professor at the railway station?' asked Iris. '*You* said that it was impossible to know which of two people was telling the truth.'

'Yes, I remember.'

'The professor pointed out two women. One was an Englishwoman in a raincoat. The other was a girl with red lips and dark hair.'

'I remember *her*. Pretty woman, like a soft black fruit.'

'But the professor said he would never believe her. That's exactly what has happened now. He won't believe *me*. He believes the others because they're middle-aged. It's not fair. *You* said it wasn't fair. So you must believe me now.'

'All right. I'll believe you. What can I do?'

'Can I tell you the story, and try to get it clear?'

He listened carefully as Iris told the story of her meeting with Miss Froy.

'I'll tell you one thing,' he said at the end. 'Miss Froy was right about the man she worked for. I think I know who he is. He's in trouble at the moment, about lots of things. Now people are saying that he's murdered a newspaper owner. It was because the newspaper said things against him.'

He picked up a thin yellow newspaper.

'It's in here,' he explained. 'But he was away at his country house when the newspaper man was murdered.'

'But it proves me right,' cried Iris in great excitement. 'I knew about the man she worked for. So Miss Froy must have told me. And there's something else. The baroness was listening when I told Miss Froy about my sunstroke. That was the only way she could know about it. So Miss Froy *was* there in the carriage with me.'

She looked so pleased that Hare hated to make her unhappy again.

'That only proves that Miss Kummer was there. *She* told you about the man she worked for. You talked about your sunstroke to *her*.'

'But what about the old parents and the dog? Surely I didn't imagine them?'

54

'Why not? Don't you ever dream?'

'I suppose so,' said Iris unhappily. 'Yes, you must be right.'

'The vicar said Miss Kummer was the lady who ordered the tea, too. My father and all my uncles are vicars. You must agree that vicars usually tell the truth.'

'Yes,' said Iris quietly.

'And that vicar has such a wonderful face,' continued Hare. 'Like God's good man.'

'But he never saw Miss Froy,' said Iris. 'He was speaking for his wife.'

Hare laughed loudly.

'You're right,' he said. 'That shows that we can all make mistakes.'

'If you were wrong about one thing, perhaps you're wrong about another.'

'True. Let's think about it again. The baroness takes Miss Froy away. The other passengers all know the baroness, and they're afraid of her. So they agree with what she says.'

'But it seems stupid,' said Iris. 'Why did they dress someone else in Miss Froy's clothes?'

'You surprised them. You got on the train at the last minute. So at first they told you that Miss Froy was never there. But then you said some other English people saw her too. So they dressed someone else in Miss Froy's clothes.'

He seemed to believe in Miss Froy. Iris felt happier again and her thoughts went in another direction.

'Does that bit of hair always stand up?' she asked.

'Yes,' he replied. 'I'm very sorry about it. Thank you. That's the first time you've shown any interest in me.'

'Miss Froy is bringing us together, isn't she? You see, you believe in her too.'

'Well, I promised to believe in *you*. So I must believe that the man Miss Froy worked for wants to kill her. The baroness is one of his family, and the doctor is helping her.'

'You really are wonderful,' Iris told him.

'But wait. What about the English people? Do the Misses Flood-Porter always tell the truth?'

'Yes, I think they do.'

'And the vicar's wife?'

Iris waited for a moment. 'Yes, I think she does.'

'I'm sure she does. She looks a really good little woman. She said Miss Kummer was the lady who had tea with you. Don't you think we should believe her?'

'Yes, I suppose so.'

'So, all this tells us is that Miss Froy probably wasn't there. But there's one more important thing. *Why* would they want to take Miss Froy away? She wasn't a very important person. She did nothing wrong. She had no enemies.'

'No,' said Iris. 'She said she was friends with everyone.'

'Was the family angry that she was going to work for their enemies?'

'No. The man she worked for shook hands with her, and said "Goodbye", and thanked her for everything.'

'Well then, I'm afraid there's an end of Miss Froy. Do you agree?'

Iris couldn't fight any longer.

'You must be right,' she said. 'I can't go against facts. . . . But she was so real. And her old parents and the dog were real too.'

She felt as if she was killing something fresh and lively.

'You've won,' she said. 'There is no Miss Froy.'

17

It was lucky that Mrs Froy did not hear her.

She was sitting at home in the country, and talking to her friends in the sitting-room.

It was a small room, and rather dark, but comfortable. There was a pot of flowers standing in the empty fire place.

Mrs Froy was short and heavy, with grey hair. She was strong-minded, and today she was very full of life. She was excited because her daughter was really on her way home.

The postcard was above the fire place. It was a coloured

picture of mountains with white tops, against a bright blue sky. In the middle of the sky was written –

'Home Friday night. Isn't it wonderful?'

Mrs Froy showed it to her visitors.

'My daughter is a great traveller,' she said. 'Here is her latest photograph. It was taken in Budapest.'

The photograph was expensive. It showed the lower half of a small face, and a hat. The hat photographed very well.

'This is the Russian one,' continued Mrs Froy. '. . . This one was taken in Madrid, on her birthday. . . . Here she is in Athens.'

Secretly, Mrs Froy did not think any of the photographs looked like her daughter. They showed a middle-aged stranger.

'This is the best one,' she said. 'Now this really *is* Winnie.'

It showed a young girl with fair hair, before she grew up and went away.

Mrs Froy looked again at the clock. She tried to imagine Winnie, in the fast train, racing across the map of Europe. She wondered when her visitors would leave. She wanted to sit and watch the clock alone.

At last she took her visitors to the door. She did not return at once. She stood looking at the green field outside. The black shadows of the trees were growing longer.

It was rather sad and lonely. She thought of her husband.

'I wish Theodore would come home.'

He seemed to hear her wish. He appeared suddenly at the far end of the field. His tall black shape was like the tree shadows.

A large hairy dog was jumping around him. Sock saw the little grey lady by the door. He raced towards her, and ran round and round her. Then he raced back to Mr Froy.

Both of them laughed at him.

'Won't Winnie be pleased to see him?' said Mr Froy.

'I can't believe that she'll be here in two days' time,' answered Mrs Froy. 'She's such a friendly girl. I'm sure she's made some useful friends on her journey. She probably knows all the best people on the train by now. .... I wonder where she is at this moment.'

Luckily Mrs Froy did not know.

18

While Hare was talking to Iris, the professor went and sat with the Misses Flood-Porter.

'Are you being kept out of your carriage by that girl?' asked Miss Rose.

The professor explained that Iris was ill.

'Ill?' Miss Rose did not believe it. 'She was laughing when she passed, arm in arm with that young man. I hope she won't cause trouble, and make us all late at Trieste.'

'It's her dog,' explained the older sister.

Miss Rose bit her lower lip.

'Yes, it's Scottie,' she said. 'I know I'm stupid about him. But he loves me so much. He's unhappy when I'm not there.'

The professor felt more friendly.

'I'm just the same about my dog,' he told them. 'I hate travelling to different countries, because I can't take her with me.' The professor liked the sisters more and more. 'I don't know what to do about that strange young lady,' he went on. 'She is making things difficult for everyone. She was staying at the same hotel as you. .... What do you think of her?'

'Don't ask me,' said Miss Rose. 'I don't like her.'

Her sister explained.

'We know nothing about her. But she was with a crowd of terrible, badly-dressed people. They drank all day and night. The noise was terrible.'

'I understand your feelings,' said the professor. 'But was she over-excited?'

'I only know what happened by the lake yesterday. Two women were shouting at each other about a man. She was one.'

'I'm not surprised,' said the professor. 'I don't think she's telling the truth. Perhaps it's because she wants everyone to look at her. Or perhaps she's ill, as a result of sunstroke. But we must listen to what she says. We're all English.'

Miss Rose took out a cigarette. Her fingers were shaking.

'Suppose . . . she *is* telling the truth?' she asked. 'It's *not* fair for us to leave the girl behind us at Trieste by herself . . . I'm so worried, I don't know what to do.'

'I don't believe her story,' said the professor. 'But, supposing the governess really was there? We need not worry about her. She probably decided to disappear. She hasn't had an accident. Someone would have seen it.'

'Exactly,' agreed Miss Flood-Porter.

'If she is hiding,' continued the professor, 'she has some reason for it. She does not want us to search for her.'

Miss Rose looked much happier.

'I do want to get home to Scottie quickly,' she said. 'You don't think I'm acting wrongly?'

'It would be wrong to stop here because of this girl's story,' said the professor.

'Thank you, professor.' Miss Rose looked at her pink hands. 'Now I can go back to Scottie without worrying any more,' she said. 'I know you are right.'

She forgot one important thing. The professor thought that Iris imagined Miss Froy. But both the sisters really saw her.

19

Iris put Miss Froy out of her mind and began to worry about herself again. Her legs were shaky. Her head felt light and empty. She was tired because she needed something to eat.

She kept her hand on the rail, trying not to fall down.

'I mustn't be ill,' she thought, afraid. 'Max is too young to be any help. Someone will push me out at the first station. And I shall be sent to the nearest hospital.'

She remembered Miss Froy's terrible story. Or did Miss Kummer tell it to her?

She was standing in the corridor. She left Hare, because she was tired, of talking and listening. But she did not want to go back to her carriage. It was too near the doctor.

The fair haired waiter came down the corridor. Iris called to him, and he turned towards her. He recognized her, and his smile disappeared. He looked away from her. He seemed about to run away.

But he listened, as she gave him her order.

'I'm not going to the restaurant for dinner,' she told him. 'I want you to bring me something in my carriage. A cup of soup. Nothing heavy. Do you understand?'

'Oh yes, madame.'

But he never brought the soup. . . .

A long line of passengers began to come past her, pushing her against the side of the corridor.

She looked at her watch. It was time for the first dinner.

'Only three hours now to Trieste,' she thought gladly.

The family from her carriage came past. Then the fair-haired girl passed, as cool as ice, with every hair in place.

Iris did not want to be alone in the carriage with the baroness.

But at last the large black form came in sight. The doctor was with her. He looked closely at Iris as he went past.

Iris sat down. She tried not to look at Miss Froy's empty corner. Then Hare hurried in.

'Are you coming to dinner?' he asked.

'No,' she told him. 'The waiter's bringing me some soup here.'

He looked at her.

'You do look tired. Let me get you a drink. No? . . . Well then, let me tell you something amusing. I was on my way here. Then suddenly I felt a woman's hand on my arm. I turned, and looked straight into the beautiful eyes of the vicar's wife. "Can you do something for me?" she asked. So of course I said "Yes".'

'What did she want?' asked Iris, without interest.

'She wants me to send a telegram for her as soon as we get to Trieste. Now this is the amusing bit. She said I mustn't tell her husband about it.'

'Oh.'

'Sorry. You really are tired, aren't you? I won't worry you any more.'

He left the carriage. Then he put his head in again.

'Do you know who Gabriel is?' he asked.

'No,' said Iris.

'I see. You clearly *don't* know anything about it.'

Time passed. The waiter did not come. This was because he did not really understand English. He knew a few English words. But he could not understand English spoken by a Briton. He always said, 'Yes, madame,' and hurried away.

Before the other passengers returned to the carriage, Iris had another visitor – the professor. He took off his glasses and cleaned them as he spoke.

'Hare has been talking to me. He's worried about you. Of course, you are not ill . . . that is not *really* ill. But are you well enough to continue the journey alone?'

'Of course I am,' cried Iris, afraid. 'I'm perfectly all right.'

'But supposing you become ill later? It will be very difficult for everyone. I have been talking to the doctor. He has a very good idea.'

He waited. Iris's heart began to jump. She knew what he was going to say.

'The doctor is taking the sick person to a hospital in Trieste,' continued the professor. 'He says he will take you too. Then you will be safely looked after for the night.'

20

'I will not go anywhere with the doctor,' said Iris.

'But . . .'

'I refuse to talk about it.'

The professor began to argue.

'No one can make me go with that doctor,' she said again.

'Then there is nothing more to be said.'

The professor was glad to go. The girl refused to be helped and he could do no more. There was time for a smoke before the second dinner.

Iris did not like the professor's face. But his back looked British and safe. And she was sending him away.

Suddenly she called him back.

'I won't go with that doctor,' she said. 'He's like death. But . . . supposing I *do* get ill . . . I'd go with *you*.'

Now two people in the carriage were afraid.

'That is impossible,' said the professor sharply. 'The doctor is being kind and helpful. It would be right to go with him.'

She shook her head. I'll never go, unless they force me, she thought.

It was a worrying thought. She seemed to have no real friends. Hare really cared about her. But why did he make that stupid joke about Mrs Barnes and a man called Gabriel?

I wish Miss Froy was here now, thought Iris. I'd feel safe with the little governess. Now Iris felt frightened, ill, helpless.

Other people on the train were feeling worse than Iris. One was the sick person in the next carriage. She was drugged, and hardly knew anything. But sometimes thoughts, and fears, came into her mind.

'Where am I? What is going to happen to me? Where are they taking me?'

Luckily these thoughts soon died down again. So she was

luckier than Mrs Barnes. Mrs Barnes was feeling terrible the whole time.

It all began when she saw the letter at the hotel desk. She knew her mother's writing at once.

'I don't want to worry you on your long journey,' wrote that good lady. 'But I'm afraid Gabriel is not well. It's nothing very bad. He is quite comfortable, and the doctor says he is doing well. So there is no need for you to worry.'

Edna Barnes quickly read through the letter. He must be very ill, she thought. Sometimes a big strong baby gets ill and dies in a few hours. Perhaps he's dead already. Her heart nearly broke.

Her husband asked what was in the letter. She hid it from him. She did not want him to be as worried as she was. But she wanted to go back to England at once.

Then she had an idea. 'I'm so frightened about Miss Rose Flood-Porter's warning dream,' she told the vicar. 'Can we go back to England today?'

The vicar was surprised, but he agreed. The sisters decided to go too. The honeymoon couple were leaving on that day as well. So everyone left the hotel.

For the first time, Edna Barnes was glad that her husband was train-sick. While he sat with closed eyes, she did not need to act. At least they were on their way home. But then came the danger of waiting at Trieste.

She meant to do the right thing. She wanted to help Miss Froy. But people told her that Miss Froy was in no danger.

The girl was just over-excited. But Gabriel was ill. He needed her, and he won.

So she agreed that Miss Kummer was Miss Froy. Then she suddenly had an idea. She asked Hare to send a telegram to the vicar's mother. She wanted her to send the answer to Calais. 'Then I'll tell my husband,' she thought. He still knew nothing. She smiled.

Only a mother knows, she thought.

Mrs Froy thought exactly the same. She was sitting in the evening light, waiting for her child's return.

63

21

Usually, Mrs Froy was a happy person. But this evening the long black shadows of the trees seemed to reach into her mind. She felt low.

I shall be glad when Winnie is safely home, she thought. Supposing she is taken ill on the journey? Anything could happen to her . . . a crash, or even worse. You read of terrible things which happen to girls travelling alone. Not that Winnie was really a girl . . . but she was so young for her age.

At this point Mrs Froy decided not to be foolish.

'Only two more nights,' she told herself. 'You ought to be as happy as a queen.'

She went out of the room and down the stairs, in search of her husband.

She found him sitting in the dark.

'Why haven't you turned on the light?' she asked.

'In a minute.' Mr Froy's voice was unusually lifeless. 'I've been sitting and thinking. A bad idea. . . . It's strange. Winnie has been away so often. But this is the first time I've ever felt afraid about her safety. I suppose I'm growing old. The ground is pulling me.'

Mrs Froy's heart gave a sudden jump as she listened. So he, too, could hear the warning voice.

Without speaking, she turned on the light. Then she looked at her husband's face.

It was white and bony – the face of a man who was ready to lie in the cold ground.

'Never talk to me like that again,' she cried angrily. She closed the green window-curtains and shut out the darkness. Her husband's face looked better in the warm light.

'Where is Sock?' she asked.

'My dear, he's waiting outside until it's time to meet

the train. He doesn't understand that it isn't Friday yet.'

'I'll make him understand,' said Mrs Froy. 'Sock.'

The big dog came in at once.

'Look darling,' said Mrs Froy. 'Winnie's not coming to-night. She's not coming tomorrow night. She's coming on *Friday* night.'

Sock's brown eyes looked up at her through his hair.

'He understands,' said Mrs Froy. 'I can always talk to animals. I know what's in his mind. He's trying to make the time pass quicker.'

22

Mrs Froy wasn't the only one who wanted the time to pass more quickly. Some of them were on the fast train, speeding towards Trieste.

One of them was Mrs Todhunter. She hid her feelings. Other women always wanted to be like her. She seemed to have everything – beauty, fashionable clothes, a rich, good-looking husband.

But her real husband was a fat, middle-aged builder. And now she wanted very much to get home to him.

Mrs Laura Parmiter lived in a beautiful new house, with everything modern. She had every comfort, plenty of money and love from her husband, and two large children.

But she was not really happy. She wanted more. Then she met a successful lawyer.

He loved her – for a time – because of her beauty, and be-cause she was interested in good books. They met a few times in London. Then he carried her away on an adventure of love. He was a king and she was a queen.

But Mrs Laura knew what she was doing. She wanted to leave her husband and marry him. There would be a difficult time. But then she would become the beautiful wife of a great

lawyer. The world soon forgets – and her husband would let her keep the children.

But the plan did not work.

The lawyer's wife was old, but she was very rich. Mrs Laura discovered that the lawyer did not wish to leave her.

Mrs Laura hid her feelings. After all, the adventure taught her one thing. A lawyer is not very different from a builder in the early morning.

So she decided to cut short the holiday, and get back to her husband as quickly as possible.

Her husband thought she was in Turin. He was on holiday in the Shetlands. Now she looked forward to seeing him again.

The Todhunters sat in their carriage, waiting for the second dinner. Everyone looked in at them as they passed down the corridor.

They were still calling themselves Todhunter. The lawyer was careful not to sign his own name. It was 'Brown'. The name of 'Sir Peveril Brown', was well-known, and his picture was often in the newspapers.

Mrs Laura kept looking at her watch.

'Still hours and hours,' she cried. 'We shall never get to Trieste, let alone Turin.'

'Can't you wait to leave me?' asked Todhunter, surprised.

'I'm not thinking of you. ... But children get ill – and husbands sometimes run away. The world is full of pretty girls.'

'But supposing he heard about *you*?'

She jumped.

'There's no chance of it, is there?' she cried sharply.

'I think we're safe,' he told her. 'But it was unlucky that there were other English visitors at the hotel. Of course no one will ever know about us. But do you remember when that girl asked us about the woman who looked in at the window? I had to think quickly then.'

'Why?' asked Laura.

'Why? Because she's disappeared. Supposing I said I saw her? The police would question me at Trieste.' Todhunter laughed. 'Can't you imagine the newspapers? "Englishwoman

lost on train." Photograph of Mr Todhunter on his holiday . . .
The English papers would soon know who I am, because I'm
too well-known.'

This gave Mrs Laura a new idea. Perhaps the game was not
lost, after all. Supposing I went to the professor and told him
that I saw Miss Froy?

Her dark blue eyes suddenly shone. Photograph of Mr Todhunter and his beautiful wife. She always photographed so
well.

His wife will leave him, she thought. Then he'll have to
marry me. I shall be the second 'Lady Brown'.

23

Mrs Laura sat and looked at the dark window. She could see
her own face mirrored, with shadowed eyes and smiling lips.
She was full of hope.

Miss Froy was full of hope too. She was in great danger.
But she still hoped that she would get home safely in the end.

Miss Froy loved her home. But she also loved to travel. She
liked new places, new sights, new people.

She enjoyed her job for the first six months. It was very
exciting. The castle was so large, with endless stone stairs, and
big mirrors everywhere. The mirrors made the castle look
twice as large as it really was.

It was such a beautiful country too. She tried to describe it
in letters to her family. The blue and purple mountains, with
white tops crashing through the sky, the racing rivers, the
rich green valleys.

'There aren't enough words,' she wrote. 'It's all wonderful.'

But after six months it was less exciting. She no longer got
lost in the castle. And she knew where the mirrors were, so it
didn't look so big. And there were insects in the carpets and
rich curtains.

Her grand bedroom was too big. It was uncomfortable and cold. The fire was not big enough. She wanted to get back to a small stone house in the country. She was tired of mountains and rivers. She wanted English fields and trees.

She was so excited that she could not sleep, on the night before her return. Her suitcases were all ready, but she still couldn't believe it.

As she lay awake, she heard the night train. It called to her, as it called to Iris later. She jumped out of bed and ran to the window. She saw it racing down the valley, a line of golden lights in the dark.

Tomorrow night *I* shall be in a train too, she thought.

She looked forward to the long journey. At last I shall get to a quiet little station in the middle of the fields, she thought. Father will be waiting in the road outside, with Sock. But I shan't reach the end of the journey till I run through the dark garden. The light will be shining out through the open door. Mother. Her eyes filled with tears.

Then a sudden fear touched her heart.

I've never wanted to go home so much before, she thought. 'Is it a warning? Suppose . . . suppose something happens . . . to keep me from getting home.'

Something happened . . . something so terrible that she really could not believe in it.

At first she was sure that someone would soon save her. How lucky it was that I met that nice English girl, she told herself. That girl will pull the train to pieces, wheel by wheel, to find me.

But time went on, and nothing happened. She remembered that the girl had sunstroke. She was not well. Perhaps she was really ill by now. And she didn't speak the language.

Something even worse was possible. Perhaps Iris tried to help, but was caught as well. Miss Froy's lips shook with fear at the thought.

Then, suddenly, she felt the train slowing down. It stopped, with a loud noise.

They've missed me, she thought. Now they are going to search the train.

And once again she saw the lights of home shining through the open door.

At that moment, the professor was standing in the corridor just outside Mrs Laura's carriage. If she called to him, Miss Froy would be saved.

There was plenty of time before they reached Trieste. She waited. Was this really a good idea? Yes. Her mind was made up.

'What are we stopping for?' she asked. She looked out and saw the lights of a station.

'What is that fool doing?' cried the lawyer. Hare was racing off to send Mrs Barnes's telegram to Bath, England. 'He's making the train late.' He looked at his watch.

To his surprise, Laura did not mind about it.

'Does it matter?' she said. 'We will get there.'

'Perhaps we shall miss the next train. I've just thought of something. Shall we leave each other before we get to Italy? We don't want to meet anyone who knows us.'

'What do you want to do?' said Mrs Laura.

'I'll take the Trieste – Paris train. Will you be all right by yourself at Milan?'

'Perfectly. I can look after myself.'

The professor went back to his carriage. Laura stood up. She was ready to follow him. But she waited.

'What's the matter?' asked the lawyer.

Laura smiled. She held the winning card.

'I'm wondering if I shall like the name of "Brown",' she said, 'after being Mrs Parmiter.'

'Will that happen?'

'Well, if your wife leaves you, you must marry me. It's the right thing to do, isn't it, darling?'

'But, my sweet, my wife won't leave me.'

'I'm not so sure. Your wife will read about us in the news-papers.'

The lawyer realized the danger which lay behind her smiles.

'Perhaps your husband will leave *you*,' he said coldly. 'But I can tell you one thing. There is already one Lady Brown. . . . My wife will never leave me.'

Laura looked at him. She couldn't believe it.

'You mean, she wouldn't mind about us?'

'My wife and I understand each other perfectly. We shall never leave each other.'

He's won, after all, she thought. I nearly made a terrible mistake, she thought. I nearly lost my husband, my beautiful house, perhaps even my children, for nothing. Thank God I talked to him first.

Mrs Laura would not now speak to the professor. She was saved. But Miss Froy was not.

The train moved slowly on. When it stopped, Miss Froy's hopes were high. Her hopes moved up out of the night into the sunshine. Then the hopes slowly disappeared. Then the train moved on, and she fell back into the dark again.

The train raced on.

24

Iris was sitting in her corner seat. The window was wet and dirty. She couldn't see anything through the glass, except sometimes a line of lights, as they raced through a small station.

Travellers think only about themselves, she thought. Those Miss Flood-Porters, and the professor don't want to trouble themselves about me or Miss Froy.

She straightened herself. Her back was hurting, and so was her neck. She wanted to rest in a comfortable bed, away from the noise of the train.

That was what the doctor said – a good night's rest.

Hare entered, and sat down in Miss Kummer's seat.

'Well?' he asked hopefully. 'Are you going to stop at Trieste?'

'No,' answered Iris.

'But are you well enough to go on?'

'Why do you worry about me?'

'I don't know.'

Iris smiled. She could not forget Miss Froy. But she felt better when Hare was there. It was exciting to be alone with him on the same terrible journey.

'You'll soon be home,' he said, 'back with your crowd of friends.'

'I don't want any of them,' she said. 'I don't want to get back. I've no home. And nothing seems worth doing.'

'What do you do with yourself?'

'Nothing. . . . Oh, I play about.'

'With other people?'

'Yes. We all do the same things. Stupid things. There's not one real person among us. Sometimes I get frightened. What's at the end of it all?'

Hare did not try to answer the question. Instead he looked out at the darkness with a half-smile. Then he began to talk about himself.

'My life's different from yours. I never know where I'm going next. But it's always rough. And things happen. Not always nice things. . . . But I could take you with me on my next job. You'd get a complete change. Not very comfortable, but interesting.'

'It sounds lovely. . . . Are you asking me to marry you?'

'No. I'm just getting ready to hide when you throw something at me.'

'But lots of men ask me to marry them. And I'd like to go to a rough place.'

'Good. Have you got any money?'

'Some. Not very much.'

'Fine. I've got none.'

They hardly knew what they were saying. Their eyes told a different story from their light words.

'You know,' said Hare at last, 'all this is stupid. I'm just trying to take your mind off things.'

'You mean – Miss Froy?'

'Yes.'

To his surprise, Iris changed the subject.

'Have you got a good brain?' she asked.

'Fairly good.'

'Could you write a detective story?'

'I suppose so.'

'Show me then. You've been very clever in proving that Miss Froy wasn't there. But supposing she was there? Tell me what could have happened to her.'

Hare began to laugh.

'I always thought that, if I liked a girl, she would be more interested in some good-looking man. I didn't think she'd be more interested in an old governess. I bit a governess once, long ago. . . . Well, let me think.'

Iris watched him with great interest. When he was thinking, the lines of his face grew harder. He looked a different man. Sometimes he ran his fingers through his hair, and it stood up even more.

'I've got it,' he said at last, with a laugh. 'Would you like to hear a new story called "The Strange Disappearance of Miss Froy"?'

'I'd love to,' she told him.

'Do you remember when you first got on the train? Was there one nurse in the next carriage, or two?'

'I only noticed one when we passed the carriage. She had a terrible face.'

'I need a second nurse for my story.'

'There *was* a second one. I met her in the corridor.'

'Have you seen her since?'

'No. But there are so many people on the train.'

'The nurses are very important for my story.'

'Yes. Go on.'

'I haven't really started yet. Well, Miss Froy is a spy. She knows something important. So she must be murdered. And a train is the best place.'

'You mean, they've thrown her out on the rails?' asked Iris weakly.

'Don't be stupid. And don't look so white. If they threw her on the line, her body would be found. Questions would be asked. No, she must *disappear*. It's difficult to prove that someone is missing on a train. At first her family will think

that she never got on the train. Or perhaps she stopped at Paris for a day or two to shop. So they will waste a lot of time before they start to search for her.'

'But they won't know what to do. They're old.'

'But even if they did, they would just meet a wall of silence.'

'Why? Is the whole train full of criminals?'

'No,' said Hare. 'Only the baroness, the doctor and the two nurses are criminals. But the other people in the baroness's carriage will do what she tells them. They won't dare to argue with her.'

'How about the railway people themselves?'

'Yes, that's true. Someone from the railway made sure that Miss Froy didn't get a seat. The baroness was probably behind that too. Then she asked Miss Froy to sit in her carriage. It's right at the end of the train.'

'It's next to the doctor's carriage, too. ... But what's happened to her?'

Iris was holding her hands closely together.

'Ah,' said Hare smiling. 'That is where I use my great brain. Miss Froy is lying in the next carriage to this. She's covered with blankets and bandages.'

'How? When?'

'You went to sleep. Then the doctor came in. He asked Miss Froy if she could help him with something. He asked her to come to the next carriage.'

'Of course she'd go.'

'Well, she goes to the carriage and gets a terrible surprise. It's completely dark. Then the three of them jump on her.'

'The three?'

'Yes. The sick person is one of them. They hold her, and the doctor gives her a drug to keep her quiet.'

Iris pictured it.

'It *could* happen,' she said.

Hare gave her a broad smile.

'I wish you could always listen to my stories. You're such a good listener. One of the nurses is a man, of course.'

'I believe she is,' said Iris.

'Well, Miss Froy is now down and out. So they tie her up

73

and bandage her face, and put a blanket over her. The first "sick person" now becomes the second nurse. She was dressed as a nurse under the blanket.'

'I saw a second one in the corridor,' agreed Iris.

'But by now you've found some English people who remember Miss Froy. So they need someone to play the part of Miss Froy. They quickly close the curtains again. Then the second nurse dresses herself in Miss Froy's clothes.'

Iris remained silent.

'It's not very good,' he said, 'but it's the best I can do.'

'What will happen to her when they reach Trieste?'

'Oh, my readers will love this bit,' explained Hare. 'They'll drive her off to some house in the country, near to some deep water. Then they'll tie weights on her and drop her in. . . . Here, what's the matter?'

Iris jumped to her feet and tried to open the door.

'Perhaps everything you say is true,' she cried. 'We mustn't waste time. We must do something.'

Hare forced her back to her seat.

'It's just a story,' he said.

'But I must get to that sick person,' she cried. 'It's Miss Froy. I must see for myself.'

'Don't be a fool. The sick person in the next carriage is *real*. And she's had a bad accident. If we force our way into that carriage, the doctor will send us out again. And quite right, too.'

'Then you won't help me?'

'Certainly not. Remember your sunstroke. It's just a story. *I really don't believe it.*'

25

'Of course,' agreed Iris slowly, 'It's just a story. What a fool I am.'

She heard a strange, very loud voice coming from down the corridor. The words meant nothing to her. But Hare's face brightened.

'Someone's got a radio,' he said, jumping up. 'It's the news. I'll be back in a minute.'

He returned, and told Iris what he heard.

'Do you remember the man that Miss Froy worked for?' he asked. 'Well, he didn't murder the newspaper owner, after all. The newspaper owner was shot in the middle of the night. But Miss Froy's gentleman left for his country house just after dinner.'

Something passed through Iris's mind, and disappeared again. Hare looked at his watch.

'Nearly time for the second dinner,' he told her. 'Are you coming?'

'No.'

When he was gone, Iris felt very tired. The train was very noisy.

Suppose – at this very minute – a dead body is being thrown out of the train, she thought.

She held her hands closely together. She began to think about the facts.

The other people in the carriage all know the baroness, she thought. Is that just chance? Or is it because she can force them to agree with what she says? Why did they not pull the curtains in the sick woman's carriage? Was it because they wanted everyone to see her? The best way to hide something is to put it where everyone can see it.

But *why* do they want to take Miss Froy away? That was

what Hare said – Why? She didn't do anything wrong. The important man she worked for was pleased with her. He thanked her.

Suddenly Iris caught her breath.

That was *why*, she said in a low voice.

He was supposed to have gone to his country house by the time of the murder. But Miss Froy saw him in the middle of the night. She knows that he didn't leave then.

So she was a danger to him.

Everyone knew that she talked a lot. And she was coming back the next year, to teach the children of his enemy.

But I can't prove any of this, she thought. Perhaps I'm imagining it all. . . . I do wish I could be sure.

Her wish came true in a strange way. The carriage was hot. Water was running down the inside of the window.

Iris watched a water drop running down the dirty glass. Suddenly she jumped. She saw that a little name was written on the glass.

She moved nearer and tried to read it.

It was 'Winifred Froy'.

26

Iris looked at the name. She could hardly believe her eyes. The writing was like a schoolgirl's.

It proves that Miss Froy sat in that corner seat. *I* was right, after all, thought Iris excitedly. But then her happiness disappeared.

She was no longer fighting shadows. She was facing real danger.

Miss Froy was in terrible danger. And she, Iris, was the only person on the train who realized it. Time was running out. She looked at her watch. It was ten minutes past nine. They would arrive at Trieste in less than an hour.

The train was racing on at a great speed. The carriages were shaking about.

Iris jumped up, but fell back again. Her head hurt when she moved and she felt very sick. She lit a cigarette.

She heard voices in the corridor. The other passengers were returning from dinner. The family, and the fair-haired girl, came first. They were all very happy after their meal. They took no notice of Iris.

They were followed by the woman who wore Miss Froy's clothes. Iris asked herself if she really was the second nurse.

They both had black eyes, a yellow skin, and bad teeth. But she wasn't sure. Iris stood up and went into the corridor.

The large black form of the baroness stood in her way. Iris's legs began to shake. Her head felt weak. The train was shaking and crashing on. She was afraid that she was going to fall.

'Let me pass, please,' she said weakly.

The baroness did not move. Instead, she looked at her face.

'You are ill,' she said. 'That is not good. You are young, and you are travelling without friends. I will ask the nurse for something to make you feel better.'

'No, thank you,' said Iris. 'Please, will you stand on one side?'

The baroness took no notice. She shouted to the hard-faced nurse.

The glass of the sick person's window was growing wet from the heat. Iris tried to look inside. The form lying on the seat seemed to have no face – only a white shape.

She asked herself what lay underneath the bandages. The nurse noticed her interest. Suddenly the nurse reached forward and held Iris's arm. Iris was being pulled inside.

Iris looked up at the hard mouth, and the dark shadow round the lips. The strong fingers were covered with short, black hairs.

It *is* a man, she thought.

Iris was filled with fear. She did not know what she was doing. She put the end of her lighted cigarette against the back of the nurse's hand. Surprised, the nurse took her hand away with a cry.

Iris quickly pushed past the baroness and hurried down the corridor.

They won't listen to me, she said to herself. But I *must* make them understand. . . . This train seems a mile long. I'll never get there . . . Miss Froy . . . I must be in time.

She seemed to be caught in some terrible dream. Heavy weights seemed to be tied to her legs. Passengers stood in her way. Miss Froy was going to be murdered, but no one cared about anything except dinner.

At last she reached the restaurant. She heard the sound of voices. She stopped in the doorway.

They were drinking their soup. They all looked very hungry. I shall never be able to get them away from their dinner, thought Iris.

She moved down the carriage. The professor looked up and saw her. He was sitting with Hare, and talking to the doctor.

They all looked at her in silence. Even Hare's eyes held no welcome. He watched her with a worried look.

Iris turned to the professor.

'Do go on drinking your soup. Don't stop – but please listen. This is very important. I know there *is* a Miss Froy. I know they're trying to murder her. And I know *why*.'

The professor gave her a tired look and continued to drink his soup. Iris told him her story. It sounded very weak. She knew that he didn't believe her. He listened silently.

At the end, he looked at the doctor. The doctor began to speak in a hurried voice. Then Hare broke in.

'That's not her story, it's mine. I told it to her. So if anyone's mad, it's—' He stopped. But Iris was too excited to notice what he meant.

'Won't you come now?' she asked the professor.

A waiter put an empty plate in front of him, ready for his fish.

'Can't it wait until after dinner?' he said in a tired voice.

'*Wait*? Can't you understand? It's terribly important. When we reach Trieste it will be too late.'

Again the professor looked at the doctor. The doctor was looking hard at Iris. At last he spoke, in English.

'Perhaps we had better come at once to see the sick woman. I'm sorry to make you wait for your dinner. But the young lady is very over-excited. It will be – safer – to try to please her.'

Once more they followed each other down the shaking corridors. Hare turned and said to Iris, in a tired but angry voice.

'Don't be a fool and do anything stupid.'

But it was too late. The nurse was already showing her burnt hand to the doctor and the professor.

Then the doctor turned to her and spoke in a very sweet voice.

'My dear young lady, did you really need to burn my poor nurse? She was only trying to help you.'

Iris realized that she was losing the game. It was time to attack. She spoke up bravely.

'I'm very sorry about the burn,' she said. 'But there is so much that I cannot understand.'

'Such as—?'

'Where is the other nurse?'

The doctor was silent for a few moments before he answered.

'There is only one nurse.'

She looked at his hard face, half-hidden behind his black beard. It's useless, she thought. I'm the only one who saw the second nurse. And the name written on the glass, no one will believe that either.

The doctor spoke to the professor.

'The young lady believes some very terrible things,' he said. 'We must make her understand that she *imagines* them.'

He went over to the covered form of the sick person. He lifted the corner of the blanket to show the feet.

'Do you recognize the shoes?' he asked.

Iris shook her head. 'No, but if you lift a corner of the bandages I shall recognize her face.'

'Ah,' said the doctor. 'I see that you do not understand. I must tell you something that is not pretty. Listen.' He touched the bandaged face lightly with his fingers. 'There is

no face here at all. *No face.* The skin is all gone. Perhaps we shall make another face, if we are lucky.'

He smiled at Iris.

'I don't believe you,' Iris told him. 'It's not true.'

'If you do not believe me, lift the bandages yourself. But I must warn you. If you do it, the blood will start to run again, and the sick woman will die at once. You will kill her. . . . But you are sure that you know the face under the bandages. Do not wait. Pull off the bandages.'

Iris felt Hare's fingers closing over her arm. She didn't believe the doctor. Here was a chance to save Miss Froy's life.

But she thought of the face with no skin on it, the rivers of blood. It was too terrible.

'I . . . I can't,' she said at last.

'Ah,' said the doctor, 'you talk, but you are not brave.'

27

The professor was talking about dinner again.

'Hurry back to the restaurant, Hare,' he said. 'Perhaps there's still some fish left.'

Hare turned to Iris.

'Do you mind?' he asked.

She gave a little laugh. 'Do go back,' she said. 'Nothing matters except dinner, does it?'

Iris shook her head. I can do nothing more for Miss Froy at the moment, she realized. The important thing is not to let people think I am mad. I'm the only person who believes in Miss Froy. So I must remain free.

The professor was leaving the carriage. Iris's brain cleared.

'Professor,' she said. 'Supposing that you get back to England, and then you read about a missing Englishwoman – Miss Froy. It will be too late to save her then. You will remember that for the rest of your life.'

'Yes, that's true,' said the professor. 'But I don't think I shall.'

'But if you will do one little thing, you will not need to be sorry at all. And you won't need to miss your dinner.'

'What do you want me to do?'

'Go with the doctor to Trieste hospital. Watch him take the bandages off.'

The professor was very surprised. But he thought carefully.

'*I* can do nothing,' Iris continued. 'I can't pull the bandages off. I'm not mad. I don't want to kill someone. And the doctor would never really let me. You know that.'

For the first time, the professor began to wonder about the doctor. Perhaps I ought to do what she says, he thought. He always tried to do the right thing.

But there were problems. The first problem was money. He was short of money. And if he stayed at Trieste he would need to buy a new railway ticket to finish his journey. It cost less if he travelled the whole journey at the same time.

Also he was going to visit an important person, when he got back to England. If he got back on Saturday instead of Friday he would be too late. He did not want to miss the visit.

The doctor watched him closely.

'Is it difficult for you to stop at Trieste?' he asked.

'Very difficult.'

'I am sorry. I would like you to do as the young lady asks.'

'Why?' asked the professor angrily.

'Because I am sure that there is some reason for the young lady's trouble. It is always "Miss Froy". Are many people in England called "Froy", like "Smith"?'

'I have never heard of it before.'

'But she has heard it before. Something terrible probably happened to her in the past. Something about a Miss Froy. She remembers the name, but she has forgotten what happened.'

'That's not true,' cried Iris. 'I won't—'

'Be quiet,' said Hare, in a quiet, angry voice. He was listening closely to what the doctor said. Perhaps this was the answer to the mystery.

'I would like you to come with me to the hospital,' continued the doctor to the professor. 'Then you will be sure that I am not hiding anything.'

'It's a stupid idea,' said the professor. The doctor wants me to go with him, thought the professor. That proves that the doctor is not a criminal. 'I think we are making too much of this,' he added.

He turned away, and started back to his dinner.

Iris was mad with anger. Hare was trying to keep her quiet by holding onto her arm.

'It's no good,' he said. 'Come away quietly.'

Iris took no notice. Instead, she shouted something.

'*Miss Froy*. Can you hear me? Hold up your hand if you can.'

28

Miss Froy heard her. She held up her hand.

She could not see, because of the bandages. But she could hear Iris's voice among the other sounds. She realized that people were talking, but she could not hear them very well. Their voices seemed a long way away, as if they were speaking on the telephone.

Her upper arms were tied to her body with bandages. And her legs were tied together.

But her hands were free. There were not enough bandages to tie them. She could move them weakly. Miss Froy's heart jumped with joy. She knew that the clever girl would see her hand move.

So she opened her fingers and held them in the air.

Then once again her mind closed over. She could not think properly because of the drugs. But sometimes her brain cleared and she remembered that terrible moment.

She remembered sitting in her carriage, when the doctor came in.

'Can someone help me to lift the sick person?' he asked. 'She cannot get any rest, and the nurse has gone out for a minute.'

Of course Miss Froy offered to help. She always wanted to help. And she was interested in the sick person. She wanted to learn more about the accident, so that she could tell her family the story.

They went into the sick person's carriage. The doctor asked her to lift the head, while he lifted the body.

Miss Froy moved towards her kindly. Poor thing, she thought. She's sick, and I'm well and happy. I'm going home.

Suddenly two long white arms shot out and took hold of her neck.

She had a moment of terrible fear, then everything went black. She knew no more.

Then things began to come back to her. She found that she was tied up. She could not see or cry out. She could hear voices talking about her.

She did not know why this was happening. But she learned what was going to happen at Trieste. She would never reach the hospital.

But she never gave up hope. She was like her Aunt Jane. This Victorian lady wished for many things. None of her wishes ever came true. But Aunt Jane never gave up hope.

But luckily Miss Froy's clear moments were short. Most of the time she was in a drugged dream. She dreamed that she was trying to get home.

She always got to the garden, and saw the light shining from the front door. The grass and flowers were brightly coloured in the light.

She was so near, but she knew that something was wrong. She could never reach the door. . . . She was dreaming about this when she heard Iris calling her name, and telling her to hold up her hand.

But she did not realize how long her brain took to understand. The doctor was pushing all his visitors out into the corridor before she began to lift her hand. And by then it was too late.

The curtains were drawn. No one except the nurse saw the weakly moving fingers.

'That was a terrible thing to do,' said the doctor. His voice shook with anger. 'I was wrong to let you in at all. But I never thought that you would try to hurt the poor woman.'

Iris was afraid of his anger. He turned to the professor.

'You can understand, Professor, that the sick woman must have complete quiet.'

'How can she be quiet on a railway journey?' cried Iris. The train was making a terrible noise.

'That is something quite different,' explained the doctor. 'You can sleep through continuous noises. But sudden sounds wake you up. I am trying to keep the sick woman asleep.'

'I quite understand,' said the professor. 'I am sorry that this has happened.' His voice was very cold when he spoke to Iris. 'You had better get back to your carriage, Miss Carr.'

'Yes, come on,' said Hare.

Iris felt that they were all against her. Suddenly she attacked again.

'I shall go to the police as soon as we get to Trieste,' she told them.

They were brave words. But her head was hurting and her legs were shaking. She did not really think she could do it. Hare pushed her along the corridor to his carriage. The professor followed, thinking about his dinner.

They got back to Hare's carriage. Iris turned to face him.

'Are you with me or against me? Are you stopping at Trieste?'

'No,' answered Hare loudly, 'and neither are you.'

'I see. Then you didn't mean what you said about liking me – and all that.'

'I certainly meant – all that.'

'Well, if you don't come with me to the police, I'll never speak to you again.'

'Don't you realize that I'm your only friend?' he asked in an unhappy voice.

'If you were a friend, you'd prove it.'

'I wish I could. A real friend would hit you on the head to keep you quiet for the next twenty-four hours.'

'Oh, I hate you,' shouted Iris. 'Go away.'

The Misses Flood-Porter in the next carriage could hear them talking.

'That girl certainly gets some excitement out of a railway journey,' said the older sister sharply.

All this time, Miss Froy was lying flat, not moving her hands. She soon realized that no one could see her. But she heard Iris shouting about the police. That was some comfort.

Other people in the compartment heard it too. She could hear them talking about it.

'Trieste,' said a man's voice. It belonged to the doctor's driver. He was wearing nurse's clothes. 'What now?'

'We must waste no time at Trieste,' answered the doctor. 'We must drive all night, to get back to safety.'

'But ... where will you drop the body?'

The doctor mentioned a place.

'It's on our road,' he explained. 'There is no one near the river. But there are plenty of fish.'

'Good. They will be hungry. Very soon there will be no face to be recognized. What about the clothes and the suitcase?'

'We shall take them with us in the car. You must burn them as soon as we get back.'

Miss Froy's brain was not very clear. But she knew they were talking about her. She shook with fear at the thought of the black, dirty water.

But she did not really understand.

The driver was speaking now.

'Supposing someone asks about her at the Trieste hospitals?'

'We shall explain that the sick person died on the way.'

'But if they ask to see the body?'

'There will be no difficulty about that. I can easily get another woman's body. Then I will cut up the face.'

'Hum. I wish I was safely at home. There is still that girl.'

'Yes, but luckily the professor believes us. He is a good man, so he thinks that all the world is good.'

'Still I wish I was back,' continued the driver.

'There is plenty of danger,' said the doctor, 'but there is plenty of money too.'

'Will you drop the English girl in the river too?' asked the driver suddenly.

'No,' answered the doctor, 'she will not be able to make any more trouble at Trieste.'

Miss Froy heard his words. For the first time she began to lose hope. She thought of the family at home.

They were thinking of her too. They were trying to keep happy. They lit a fire, and had eggs for supper. Sock lay on the carpet and watched the fire.

Mr Froy looked at his wife. He noticed that her small mouth was tired. She's older than I am, he realized for the first time. And I, too, have grown old.

Then he looked at the clock.

'Winnie will soon reach Trieste,' he told his wife.

Mrs Froy told the dog.

'Sock, Winnie is really on her way home now. Every minute she is coming nearer . . . nearer . . . nearer. In another half-hour she'll be at Trieste.'

Trieste.

29

The waiter managed to save some dinner for the professor and Hare. They ate it in silence. They were finishing their cheese when the doctor came in and sat down at their table.

'I am sorry to trouble you,' he said, 'but I want to talk to you about the young English lady.'

'Coffee, please,' said the professor to the waiter. 'Black. . . . Well . . . what is the trouble *now*?'

'I am worried about her health. She is in danger.'

'Why?'

'She is imagining things ... she is highly excited ...'

He saw the look on Hare's face, and turned towards him.

'Excuse me. Is the young lady a friend of yours? And has she just been very angry with you?'

'Yes. I'm not very popular at the moment.'

'That is what I thought. It is a sign that the mind is sick. They attack the one they love best.'

The doctor knew that Hare was interested now.

'There is no real danger if we are careful. But her brain must be rested. She must have a long sleep. Then I am sure she will wake up quite well again.'

'What shall we do?' asked the professor carefully.

'Can we tell her to take a drug to make her sleep?' asked the doctor.

'She will never agree.'

'Then we must force her.'

'Impossible.'

'Can you trick her into taking it?'

The professor remained silent. The doctor began to stand up.

'I am a doctor. I must warn you. But you must decide.'

He was walking away. Hare called him back.

'Don't go, doctor. I feel the same as you about this.' He turned to the professor. 'Can't we do something?'

The professor's long upper lip seemed to grow longer.

'We must not trick her,' he said.

'Would you prefer to see her go mad?' asked Hare angrily.

'There is no danger of that,' the professor told them. 'I have met over-excited young women before.'

'What will you do then?' asked Hare.

'I shall speak to her.'

He finished his coffee and got up slowly. He walked along the corridors to where Iris was sitting.

She was lighting cigarette after cigarette, and throwing them away, half-smoked. The professor looked at the cigarette ends on the floor.

'Will you accept some friendly help?' he asked. He spoke as if she were a child.

'No,' answered Iris. 'I want to hear the truth, for a change.'

'You will not like the truth. But you have asked for it, so you shall have it. . . . The doctor has told me that you are sick in your mind because of your sunstroke.'

He saw fear in her eyes.

'Do you mean . . . *mad*?' she asked in a low voice.

'Oh no. Nothing to be afraid of. But he is worried about your safety because you are travelling alone. He will be forced to do something about it, unless you can keep quiet.'

'What will he be forced to do?' asked Iris. 'Do you mean the hospital? No one can make me go there against my will.'

The professor held up one finger, and spoke loudly.

'If you keep quiet, everything will be all right. But you are being very difficult. That must stop.'

The professor was not so unkind as he seemed. He thought he was doing the right thing.

He did not realize what terrible fear he was throwing her into. She was white to her lips. She moved right back into the corner of the carriage. She was afraid of him . . . afraid of everyone on the train.

She lighted one more cigarette with shaking fingers. She remembered Miss Froy's story about the woman who was taken away to a madhouse. Perhaps the same would happen to her if she continued to try to find Miss Froy. They would say she was mad. They would take her away and shut her up. Then she really would go mad.

She realized one thing. It was dangerous to say any more about Miss Froy. She suddenly thought of England, of Victoria station, of her crowd of friends. She wanted to get home safely.

'Well?' repeated the professor. 'Do you understand me?'

'Yes,' she replied in a low voice.

'You'll make no more trouble?'

'No.'

'Good. . . . Now, will you agree that you imagined Miss Froy?'

Iris felt like a criminal when she said,

'Yes. I imagined her. There is no Miss Froy.'

30

The doctor watched the professor as he left the restaurant.

'That is a very clever man,' he said to Hare. 'He thinks he can make illness better by arguing. Perhaps he is right. I hope that I shall be proved wrong.'

He watched Hare's worried face closely. 'What do you think about it?' he asked.

'I know he's making a terrible mistake,' said the young man angrily.

'Perhaps you feel that the professor is cleverer than you?'

'No, I don't.'

'Then I do not understand why you are waiting,' said the Doctor. 'Perhaps you are afraid of the young lady's anger when she finds she has been tricked? But it is better to be angry than to go mad.'

'Don't say any more,' said Hare. 'I've got to *think*.'

'There is not much time left,' said the doctor.

'I know. But . . . it's dangerous.'

'Not at all. Here is my address. I will write a note to say that the drug will not hurt her. I will do more. I will give you some of the drug to show people in England. They will tell you that it is safe.'

Hare pulled at his lip. He knew that the doctor's offer was fair. But he was still worried.

At last the doctor looked at his watch.

'I must go back to my patient,' he said.

Hare jumped up. 'One minute, doctor. How can we give her the drug?'

The doctor knew that he was winning.

'The poor young lady has had no dinner,' he said. 'You can bring her a small cup of soup.'

'Of course,' cried Hare. 'I never thought she'd be hungry

. . . But if she is asleep, how can she change trains at Trieste?'

'The drug will not work completely until she is in the Italian train. Then she will sleep and sleep. But at Trieste she will just be very heavy, very quiet. And . . . she will be far too sleepy to worry about the imagined lady.'

'All right . . . I'll take a chance.'

The doctor went with him to the kitchen.

Soon Hare was beginning his journey along the corridors. He was holding a half-filled cup of soup.

Meanwhile Iris was having a brain-storm. She was so full of fear that she could not move. Something seemed to have broken in her brain. She could not help Miss Froy. Nothing was left.

I was her only chance, she told herself.

She tried hard to forget her. But little pictures kept appearing before her closed eyes. Two old people, standing in a lighted doorway . . . waiting. Sock – a big hairy dog – racing off to meet someone who would never come.

The thought of the dog was the worst. 'The news will probably kill both parents,' she thought. 'And then what will happen to the dog?'

Her head was hurting terribly. The noise of the train wheels seemed to be saying. 'Nearer . . . nearer . . . nearer . . . *nearer* . . . NEARER.'

Nearer to Trieste. The train was racing over the rails, shaking from side to side.

Hare entered the carriage. Iris did not look up or speak to him.

'Still hating me?' he asked.

'I only hate myself,' she said quietly.

'I've brought you some soup.'

'How sweet of you . . . but I couldn't touch it.'

'Try. It'll make you feel better.'

'All right then. Leave it, will you?'

'No. I know that old trick. As soon as I go you'll throw it out of the window. Well – I'm not going.'

Iris put her hand to her head.

'I feel so sick,' she said.

'You need something to eat.'

'Oh well . . .'

She drank the first spoonful; then she stopped. Hare watched her.

'What *is* it?' she asked. 'It's got a terrible druggy taste.'

'It's the same soup that I drank at dinner,' said Hare. He felt bad about it.

'Well, I'd better get it finished.'

She lifted the cup to her lips and drank it quickly.

'You'll feel better soon,' Hare told her. He took the empty cup from her hand.

For a time they sat in silence. He watched her carefully, waiting for the first sign of sleep. He knew that drugs act differently on different people.

If anything goes wrong, he thought, I'll be in trouble.

He could hear the professor's high voice in the next carriage. He was talking to the Misses Flood-Porter.

Iris recognized the voices.

'That's the professor, isn't it? I wish you'd tell him that he's making too much noise. Tell him he's making trouble. That's what he told me.'

Hare was surprised at her bright voice. Her eyes looked better too.

'That doctor's drug's doing no good,' he thought angrily. 'She's not getting sleepy. She's waking up. She'll be fighting-mad by the time we get to Trieste.'

In fact the food was doing her good. And the drug was quietening her brain-storm, like oil on a rough sea. For a time she felt stronger, and braver.

I shall go on fighting, she told herself.

She smiled at Hare. He smiled back at her.

I'm sorry to trick him, she thought. I shall appear quiet, and make no trouble. Then I shall get out at Trieste and take a taxi. I shall follow the doctor and the sick woman to the hospital. Then I shall race off and fetch the police.

She looked into Hare's eyes.

What a nice long sleep she'll have on the Italian train, he thought. I'm sorry to trick her.

31

They were still some way from Trieste. But passengers were beginning to get ready. They were getting their suitcases and pulling on coats and hats. The professor left the Misses Flood-Porter and entered his own carriage.

'We shall soon reach Trieste,' he said to Iris.

'I must get my suitcase,' she said.

For the last time she made the shaky journey along the train. No one took any notice of her. Suitcases and bags were standing in the corridor. Mothers were calling to children, and cleaning their chocolate-covered mouths. Newspapers were pushed under the seats.

The doctor came out of the sick person's carriage. His face looked as dry and white as dead wood, above his black beard. His eyes were like black lakes behind his thick glasses.

'Is madame better?'

'Oh yes. I'm just feeling tired. When I sit down I shan't want to move again.'

The doctor gave Hare a pleased look. She went into the carriage. No one took any notice of her. The mother and child were putting things into their suitcases. The fair-haired girl was carefully painting her face. The father was holding the baroness's bag.

Iris sat and watched them. She opened her handbag slowly, and took out her comb. She was feeling sleepy. She opened and closed her eyes, then began to comb her hair.

Before she finished, her eyes were closing again. She could not see properly. She fought to keep awake, but sleep was coming over her.

Outside, Trieste was a red light, far away on the night sky. The train was slowing down now. The driver had plenty of time.

Iris's head fell forward. Her eyes were closed. Then she heard a dog, far away, and woke up. She looked out of the window. There were lights. They were nearly into Trieste.

She thought of Miss Froy.

'Trieste,' she thought. 'I *must* keep awake.'

Then once again her eyes closed. She lay back in the corner.

Hare called to the doctor.

'How shall I get her out at Trieste?' he asked.

'You will have no trouble. She will wake at a touch. She is not deeply asleep yet.'

Hare stood in the corridor and looked out of the window. In every carriage people were taking their suitcases.

Iris slept. . . .

The Todhunters were saying goodbye.

'Shall we say goodbye now,' the lawyer asked, 'before we are in a crowd of people?'

'Goodbye,' said Mrs Laura, looking away. 'Thank you for everything. It's been a cheap holiday for me. Cheap in every way.'

In the next carriage something was terribly wrong. Miss Flood-Porter discovered it.

'Rose, did you see them put the brown suitcase on the train?'

'No.'

'Then I believe it's been left behind. It was pushed under the bed. Do you remember?'

Iris slept on.

She was dreaming of power. She dreamt that she was on her way to save Miss Froy. The corridors were hundreds of miles long. The doctor and a crowd of passengers were standing in her way. But she pushed them away. They disappeared like smoke.

Shouts and sudden lights told her that they were racing into Trieste. At once she got to her feet, half-awake, and half in a dream. She walked straight into the next compartment.

Everyone was taken by surprise. They all thought she was asleep. The doctor and his driver, in nurse's clothes, were looking out of the window. Hare saw her enter, and tried to stop her.

He was too late. Iris hurried towards the sick woman and pulled the bandages from her face. The drug made her brave enough to do the impossible thing.

Hare held his breath. But instead of blood, and terrible cuts, there was the face of a middle-aged woman.

Iris gave a low cry.

'*Miss Froy.*'

32

Two days later, Iris was standing at Victoria Station with the other passengers. The Misses Flood-Porter did not speak to her. But they were very friendly towards Mrs Barnes when she came to say 'Goodbye.' Her face was bright and happy. She found a telegram at Calais.

'Gabriel's cold has quite gone. Very well again.'

'Wasn't it *strange* about the honeymoon couple?' asked the older Miss Flood-Porter. 'He wasn't on the Venice train. And she got off at Milan . . . alone.'

'Yes,' agreed Mrs Barnes. 'My husband doesn't like me to say this. But I wonder if they were really married.'

Iris smiled to herself. She was still shaky, but she felt full of fresh life. She was glad to be back, glad to be alive. Hare was finding her suitcase. Her thoughts went back to the journey.

She could not remember some things at all. There was a complete black-out at Trieste. Then she was racing through the darkness on the Italian train. She slept most of the time.

In the morning she discovered another passenger in the carriage. It was a little middle-aged woman with a small lined face and bright blue eyes.

'Oh, Miss Froy,' cried Iris, 'you have caused me a lot of trouble.'

'I'm just making up my story to tell them at home,' said Miss Froy. 'Mother will be so excited.'

'Are you going to tell her?' asked Iris, surprised.

'Oh, not about *me*. About you. Your love-story. Is it true?'

Iris did not know herself until that minute.

'Yes,' she replied. 'I'm going with him next time.'

Hare would not tell Iris what happened at Trieste. 'Wait till we get to London,' he said.

'You must tell me now,' she said at Victoria.

They sat down, and she listened to his story.

'It wasn't very exciting. There was no fighting – nothing. The doctor and the two nurses were taken away quietly.'

'What happened to the baroness?'

'Oh, she just sailed out, twice her natural size.'

'But what did the others say when they heard about Miss Froy? After all, I was right. And everyone else was wrong except me.'

'They weren't really very interested,' said Hare. 'One of the Misses Flood-Porter's suitcases was missing at Trieste. Everyone was so worried about it that they didn't take any notice of Miss Froy.'

That evening Mrs Froy stood at the window of Winnie's bedroom. She could not see the station because of the trees. But she could see one red light.

Outside the window it was dark and silent. Then suddenly the silence was broken by the sound of a train.

Was Winnie on it? She could see nothing. Her eyes were not very good.

She held her breath. Somewhere far away she heard the sound of a large excited dog. Then she saw him racing up to the front door. He was coming to tell her that Winnie was home.

Glossary

(The glossary gives the meaning of the word as it is used in this book. Other possible meanings are not given.)

bandage long white piece of material used to cover a part of the body that has been hurt

baroness name given to the wife of a baron. A baron is the head of an old, rich, powerful family

beard hair growing on a man's face

carriage a passenger train pulls a number of carriages. Each carriage contains compartments and seats for passengers

compartment one of a number of rooms in the carriage of a passenger train

corridor a long narrow walk way on one side of the train. Passengers walk along the corridor to reach other compartments or carriages

couple a man and a woman together

drug a type of medicine used to make a person go to sleep

governess a woman who teaches the young children of a family and usually lives with them in the same house

honeymoon a holiday taken by a couple who have just got married

imagine to make a picture or idea in your mind of something or someone you cannot see

professor the head teacher at a university

sunstroke an illness caused by getting too hot in the sun

vicar a person who teaches people about God